The Fullness of Love

The Fullness of Love

From Mere Churchianity to an Awakened Life

Eric Todd

RESOURCE *Publications* · Eugene, Oregon

THE FULLNESS OF LOVE
From Mere Churchianity to an Awakened Life

Resource Publications
An Imprint of Wipf and Stock Publishers
199 W. 8th Ave., Suite 3
Eugene, OR 97401

www.wipfandstock.com

PAPERBACK ISBN: 978-1-6667-4096-7
HARDCOVER ISBN: 978-1-6667-4097-4
EBOOK ISBN: 978-1-6667-4098-1

08/22/22

Contents

Preface

RELIGION IS LIKE A finger pointing to the sun and prescribes its own brand of lessons in how to live under it. Meanwhile, the sun simply "is" and provides life-giving energy, warmth, and grace to everyone, regardless of belief. You have a choice in how to live your life. Choose to be conscripted into religion with all its trappings and constrictions, never directly experiencing the sun; choose to ignore the sun, unconsciously benefiting from its life-giving energy; or you can abide in the sun, acknowledging its presence, and fully immersed in its rays. This book points the way to soak up the sun. Cue Sheryl Crow.

Introduction

MONICA WAS A DEVOUT woman of faith with a white picket fenced in life. She painstakingly kept up appearances as a loving wife and doting mother but suffered a contentious marriage. Her man was a mid-level government bureaucrat welded to his career with a wandering eye for the . . . well maybe let's just leave it there. It was a mixed marriage 'til death did them part because throughout their relationship he showed zero interest in a relationship with God. In the end, though, Monica's prayer was answered when the love of her long-suffering life gave his heart to Jesus after tossing a Hail Mary on the fifty-yard line of his deathbed.

Her son Auggie was also a source of major disappointment. He wasted years of his life as a party boy completely saturated in a hedonistic lifestyle, then brazenly chose to openly "live in sin" for fifteen years with a woman who bore him a son. His wildly insincere prayer became a meme of sorts, "God grant me chastity and continence, but not yet."

Monica intervened in his debauched downward spiral, while actively campaigning for her son's redemption as any good Christian mom would. So, she arranged a proper marriage for Auggie with a twelve-year-old girl. Yes, your suspicion is on lock that things are not quite what they seem in this little vignette.

Introduction

A talented rhetorical speaker and educator, Auggie spent a decade dedicated to the religion of Manichaeism and a lifetime of study of neoplatonism, both which shaped his worldview before his conversion to Christ and subsequent coercion to join the Catholic priesthood. So obviously, he ultimately chose to opt out of the arranged marriage with the young girl. Props.

Today, we know Auggie as St. Augustine who lived four hundred years after Jesus taught on the hillsides of ancient Israel. He is revered as an iconic church father and developed the constructs of original sin, predestination, and the "just war theory." To Augustine, philosophy was unified with faith and not interchangeable.

One thing for sure is that family interpersonal relationships have not really evolved much in the last two thousand years (albeit in America we do not take kindly to arranged marriages with child brides, well in most states, that is).

To expand on Augustine's worldview, Manichaeism taught a dualistic cosmology describing the struggle between good and evil, represented by spiritual light and a physical world of darkness. Through an ongoing process, light was gradually removed from the material world and returned to the world of light. Built on the shoulders of earlier Mesopotamian religions and Gnosticism, its hallowed founder, "Mani," was thought to be the final prophet after Zoroaster, Buddha, and Jesus.[1]

A more enduring philosophy of the seminal constructor of Christianity was neoplatonism. In the Middle Ages, it was studied by Muslim, Christian, and Jewish philosophers alike, propagated in part by a fifth century Christian neoplatonist, Pseudo-Dionysius the Areopagite.[2] In a compelling annotation, the thirteenth century mystic Meister Eckhart was influenced by neoplatonism, propagating a contemplative way of life that promotes a unitive fusion of experiential faith. It also had a strong influence on "perennialism," which teaches that all religions at their core lead to the One True God or "The One." Influence continued through nineteenth-century universalism and postmodern spirituality and

1. New World Encyclopedia, "Manichaeism."
2. Corrigan and Harrington, "Pseudo-Dionysius the Areopagite."

nondualism. Neoplatonism is essentially the glue that bonds mystical traditions across the world.

Augustine wrote his book *Confessions* at a time when Christianity's disciples were largely peasants and the lower classes. He integrated neoplatonic philosophies and ideas, followed by the intelligentsia and upper classes to provide credibility to Christian doctrine. For further study, have a read of Shon H. Kraley's 1990 article, "Neoplatonic Influences in Augustine's Confessions."[3]

Thus, in addition to the Scriptures, Augustine's theological theories were strongly influenced by extra-biblical Middle Eastern religion and philosophy. Right or wrong, truth or heresy, it is simply a fact of history. But "sola scriptura" (literally "by Scripture alone," as the inerrant very word of God) it is not, nor is it ever, if honesty is fully explored. Every writer, teacher, or philosopher of the faith was, is, and ever shall be influenced by extra-biblical ideation, content, and experience.

Remarkably, during a great schism of the church in 1054, Augustine's more contemplative, inner work of faith was adopted by the East, which evolved to become the Eastern Orthodox Church. The West was influenced more so by Augustine's trinitarian teachings and later influenced Calvinism, which evolved to many of the tentacles of modern Evangelicalism, in which the recipe included a dash or so of other theological theories sprinkled in for good measure. Dozens of sects, some more radical than others, adopted other soteriological constructs. For example, Pentecostalism's roots are Arminian (look up Jacobus Arminius, 1560–1609 if you like), rather than Calvinistic.

St. Augustine formed the basis of the core tenets of what was to become modern western Christianity. However, over the last two hundred years or so in America, the faith of many devolved into "Churchianity," driven by religious nationalism and a worship not of Christ, but of power and a praxis of politics over love, mercy, and charity, and with roots strangled by antebellum pro-slavery.

Historically, it is clear, as we will deep dive on the subject, that followers of Christ, particularly since the Reformation and

3. Kraley, "Neoplatonic."

remarkably in America, have not truly been exposed to or fully experienced the fullness of the Gospel of the Christ. What was believed in the first few hundred years after the resurrection of Jesus was marginalized, compartmentalized, lost, or at times dismembered by wolves disguised as sheep. It began in Rome with the Papacy, splintered in 1054, as noted above, and stunningly so during the Reformation, whereby the reformers attempted to reimagine Christianity with but a fraction of the fullness of the faith's wealth of orthodoxy. Ostensibly, Protestantism reformed Roman Catholicism, but the Roman Church was and remains only one of hundreds of splintered denominations of Christianity. Five hundred years later and particularly in the West, we are left with a morality mob bereft of the truth, light, mercy, and grace Jesus commanded disciples to live by and proclaim to the world.

However, this little book is full of hope and earnestness in its exploration of the awesomeness of the God of Wonders to guide the spiritual seeker to an immersive and authentic faith. And it is 100 percent based on the beautifully radical teachings of Jesus the Christ. At scale, the byproduct of such an undertaking can exorcise religious nationalism from the church with finality and provide "The Way" (as early followers of Christ called the practice of the faith) to awaken to the fullness of love in Christ. Let's try to wrestle together through these writings because the stakes are high, and we are all accountable.

In GOP We Trust

MY NAME IS ERIC and I'm a recovering Evangelical. I've been sober now for ten years give or take. Yes, there were a few hiccups from time to time because the severing of self-righteous moral superiority sewn into a religious spine can eviscerate the host's weakened impunity system. So, it's a process. But overall, I've been clean for the better part of a decade now.

With tongue firmly planted in cheek, a lifelong struggle with alcoholism is honestly the closest analogy I can muster to my experience as a disciple of the Christ co-opted cultish religion. The hangover has mercifully passed. And I have found freedom in a faith that is no longer "churchianitized for my protection."

It did, however, take a few bourbons, many literal dark nights of the soul, and a lot of forgiveness to overcome the fact that I was defrauded of an authentic faith for three decades of my life. This book is therapeutic in approach and my prayer is that it can provide you (and me) with hope. But if you believe that this American brand of Christianity is a bottom-up cultural faith movement, you are in for a world of hurt. The sad truth: it is overwhelmingly a top-down manipulation machine of power brokers widely and not so widely known and built to rule the world. Literally.

As noted in the introduction, John Calvin, a sixteenth century Protestant reformer was highly influenced by St. Augustine. Calvinism expanded on and baked into the Christian theology the theories of original sin, substitutional atonement salvation, and predestination (sometimes at odds with free will), which is the core of modern fundamentalism.[1]

An abiding influence continued through the centuries, but cultural beliefs, racism, and politics muscled in to dominate the teachings of church leadership including Robert Lewis Darby, RJ Rushdoony, Jerry Falwell, Pat Robertson, D. James Kennedy, and a less well-known, but uber power player, Ralph Drollinger. Drollinger's "Capitol Ministries" hosts Bible studies to political leadership reaching cabinet level and includes former VPOTUS, Mike Pence. The goal is to target politicians to flagrantly influence policy with revisionist history screwed into a distorted theology that we will explore further, should you dare to read past this paragraph.

Robert Lewis Dabney, a Presbyterian minister born in Virginia circa 1820, sermonized the plight of the white folks who were taxed to support "the pretended education to the brats of black paupers." He proclaimed the "righteousness of slavery" and stated that rejecting it was "tantamount to rejecting Christianity." Dabney was not a friend to democracy either, which he referred to as "mobocracy," but had the foresight to understand that if Christians would go together to the polls, they would flip the electorate every time; a sentiment he expressed in his 1857 published article in the Central Presbyterian, "Christians Pray for Your Nation." The itinerate pro-slavery preacher believed that public education was "pagan" and that the movement that led to a woman's right to wait for it . . . vote . . . would destroy America.[2]

Why do we care about this obscure Civil War–era pastor, who, by the way, was also the biographer of Confederate leader Stonewall Jackson? Because he heavily influenced RJ Rushdoony, of whom it has been chronicled by Gary North, a Christian Reconstructionist guru, that his "writings are the source of many of

1. Elwell, *Evangelical Dictionary of Theology*, 201–3.
2. Stewart, *Power Worshipers*, 106.

the core ideas of the New Christian Right, a voting bloc whose unforeseen arrival in American politics in 1980 caught the media by surprise."[3]

Rushdoony was a pioneer of the "Dominionist" Christian reconstructionist platform which propagates the notion that the Bible proclaims Christians must dominate all of society and are mandated by God to lead the government in a return to biblical law, on which America was supposedly founded; notions that have all been discredited and void of truth by credible historians and constitutionalists which we will explore in this book.

An excerpt from an excellent blog post on the topic appeared in the "Texas Observer" by David Brockman, called, "The Radical Theology That Could Make Religious Freedom A Thing of The Past," which states:

> "Ironically, for all their talk about what those Founders intended, it seems that Dominionists have failed to heed the wisdom of two of the most prominent, Thomas Jefferson and James Madison. Madison warned that when government prefers one religion over others, religion suffers. A government that can make Christianity the official religion, he observed, can just as easily prefer one form of Christianity over others—for instance, Catholicism over Evangelicalism. For his part, Jefferson appealed to history. Whenever government officials "have assumed dominion over the faith of others, setting up their own opinions and modes of thinking as the only true and infallible" (my emphasis), he wrote, they have ended up creating "false religions."[4]

Rushdoony highly influenced the next generation of Churchianity activist leaders who refined the message and galvanized the coalescence of the faithful, through a host of widely popular televangelists and as noted earlier, many lesser-known manipulation masterminds. Among them, Ralph Drollinger, who implied

---

3. Stewart, *Power Worshipers*, 103.
4. Brockman, "Radical," para. 19–20.

that homosexuals were implicated in the wrath of God that brought on the COVID-19 pandemic.[5]

Churchianity theology requires a lot of transmuting of Scripture. Verses associated with two-thousand-year-old master/slave relationships are compared to modern day employer/employee and government/citizen alliances. This makes for convenient sermonizing against labor unions, social welfare programs, and taxes. Apparently, God hates taxes and programs that benefit the poor, discriminated, and ill. Food stamps and housing assistance are considered unbiblical, but God loves low taxation, and anything that benefits business, corporations, and the wealthy. And most definitely God is all in for rugged individualism and personal responsibility at any cost.

Let's go for broke in an overreaching, preposterous scenario to posit that a global pandemic hits, your corporate HR department head furloughs you because that is what the "market solution" lands on, you lose your home, and you can't feed yourself or your family. After all avenues of bootstrapped personal responsibility fail, who is supposed to give you a hand up according to the gospel of Churchianity? Your dad. Seriously. If you do not have a dad, then your family. If you do not have a family, then the church, but never the government. If that is truly the case, the church has failed miserably. The state assumes the role of the evil slave owner in most transmuted propaganda to control the people, while in parallel (and convenient to the cause), business owners are positioned as kindly slave masters . . . if employees do not organize, that is, otherwise the whip comes down. Thus, freedom is exclusively found in the Churchianity gospel, not the fourteenth amendment or anywhere else for that matter. Therefore, it is right and appropriate to be free spiritually, while a slave to business masters (but not government masters). Get it?

I would be remiss not to mention power brokers like the Family Research Council, a leading policy influencer group with twenty-five thousand pastor members. They endorse hyper conservative leaders, so these pastors are not politically neutral by any

5. Sopelsa, "Trump," para. 1.

means. In my humble opinion, with a bit of investigation, thousands of churches could and should lose their precious tax-exempt status. Brazen as they are, this does not seem to bother them. To paraphrase Trump, "If you're listening IRS, maybe take a look?" The FRC strategically targets fear by sowing the seeds of "us vs. them" and "good vs. evil" in its manipulation of Scripture to compel congregants to get out the vote for conservative candidates, because of course democrats are evil and full of Satan's lies.

The goal is to advance "kingdom" values, but these values overwhelmingly benefit the billionaire class; are anti-labor, homophobic, and racist; and have eviscerated the middle class as income inequality is now rampant across the US.

Further, complex racial dynamics are flummoxing their efforts because America's demographic is changing, but the tenets of Churchianity are implicitly baked into white ideals of cultural identity. Thus, there is an active recruitment of pastors of all colors, while the propagated policies promote brown and black voter suppression and draconian immigration and border policies.

The result is flabbergasting, as brown, black, and white low- and middle-income disciples of Churchianity clearly vote against their own best interest. Why? Overwhelmingly it is the seminal cause du jour of abortion. If one steps out of line and dares to question stagnant wages, income inequality, affordable housing, unionizing, the right to healthcare, systemic racism, controversial foreign policy or action, environmentalism, climate change, or any thoughtful ideation, the answer is simply that a pro-life vote trumps any other issue (ex-presidential pun intended). Otherwise, why would any right-thinking person vote against their own life, liberty, and pursuit of happiness?

But truth is not found in the far right, which by the way is not conservative, inasmuch as truth is not found in the far left, which by the way is not liberal either. These are both extremes. I'm not suggesting that the political default should always be centric, but truth, aka facts, is generally found in the center, where politicians can come together to accomplish goals that benefit the American people. And it is clear after several years of pandemic that the US government bears responsibility to provide crucial safety nets to those most vulnerable, which it turns out to be most of the population.

What might strike you as astonishing is the fact that abortion rights were never on the radar of rank-and-file believers or high-profile leaders in the wild and turbulent '60s and '70s. Abortion rights were seen in Evangelical circles in a positive light. Kindly, read that again. Scratch your head, you deserve a good one.

Historical scrutiny proves that there was zero moral outrage by Protestant Christians in response to the US Supreme Court's 1973 Roe v. Wade ruling legalizing abortion. In fact, it was not until 1979 that evangelical leaders, led by religious conservative activist Paul Weyrich, galvanized the issue of abortion to deny the "born-again" President Jimmy Carter a second term. But what was the underlying cause, if not abortion? Racial segregation.

Christian schools, including Bob Jones University, were in danger of losing their tax-exempt status due to new segregation laws signed by Republican President Nixon. "At risk" private Christian schools denied black student admission, while racist theologians touted conveniently twisted Bible verses that purportedly mandated segregation. But an issue rooted in blatant racism could not galvanize the faithful, so leadership sought to lock down an issue that would. Catholics had already taken up the mantle of abortion, so right-wing leadership suddenly got down for the cause. And it worked more than anyone could ever imagine.

But if Google existed in the '70s, a key word search would have included the words "so what" to glean any understanding of Evangelical interest in abortion rights. In 1968, the iconic Billy Graham stated, "In general, I would disagree with [the Catholic stance]," adding, "I believe in Planned Parenthood" as justification for abortion, thus pontificating that abortion was not a sin.[6] Read that sentence again, too. "The 1971 convention of the Southern Baptists endorsed a resolution calling for the legislation of abortion to preserve the 'emotional, mental, and physical health of the mother' as well as in

6. Stewart, *Power Worshipers*, 67.

the cases of rape, incest, and deformity." The SBC reaffirmed the position in 1974 and 1976 years after Roe v. Wade.[7]

"I have always felt that it was only after a child was born and had a life separate from its mother that it became an individual person . . . and it has always, therefore, seemed to me that what is best for the mother and for the future should be allowed."[8] That quote is from W. A. Criswell, a high-profile conservative leader, former president of the Southern Baptist Convention, and senior pastor of First Baptist Church in Dallas, Texas. "Religious liberty, human equality and justice are advanced by the Supreme Court abortion decision," wrote W. Barry Garrett of Baptist Press.[9]

In 1969, the first year of desegregation, Green v. Connally, not Roe v. Wade, was the actual catalyst that led conservative leadership to find an issue to consolidate the Evangelical vote. The case against US Treasury Secretary John Connally was brought by black families in Mississippi and claimed:

> Plaintiffs, Negro Federal taxpayers and their minor children attending public schools in Mississippi, brought this class action on May 21, 1969, seeking to enjoin the Secretary of the Treasury and Commissioner of Internal Revenue from according to tax exempt status to private schools in Mississippi which exclude Negro students on the basis of race or color. They sought a declaration (1) that granting tax exempt status to such schools is violative of the provisions of the Internal Revenue Code of 1954 governing charities and charitable contributions; or (2) that if granting such status is authorized by the Code, then to that extent Sections 170 and 501 of the Code are unconstitutional.[10]

Green won.

The IRS began sending racial policy questionnaires to church-sanctioned segregated academies including Liberty University

---

7. Stewart, *Power Worshipers*, 67.

8. Balmer, "Real Origins."

9. Stewart, *Power Worshipers*, 67.

10. Justia, *Green*, para. 1.

founder Jerry Falwell's Lynchburg Christian School. The infuriated Falwell claimed, "In some states it's easier to open a massage parlor than a Christian school."[11] Revisionist historians transmute his quote in the light of Christian persecution, when in fact the quote blatantly unveils Falwell's unbridled racist beliefs.

Democratic President Jimmy Carter was blamed by religious conservatives for IRS actions against segregated schools. Truth be damned, as it was clear in their dogged determination to elect a conservative and deny an openly born-again Christian Jimmy Carter another term. The truth, however, was the policy was enacted by Republican President Nixon. And Bob Jones University finally lost its tax-exempt status after years of wrangling with the IRS, but it all ended before Carter even took office.

Let's tie it all up with these quotes by religious conservative activist Paul Weyrich: "The new political philosophy must be defined by us (conservatives) in moral terms, packaged in non-religious language, and propagated throughout the country by our new coalition." And also, "When political power is achieved, the moral majority will have the opportunity to re-create this great nation."[12]

Weyrich spent twenty years throwing issues from porn to school prayer at the Evangelical wall to see what might stick to mask the religious conservative racist underbelly and build what could become a massive voting bloc—to no avail.

Enter Francis A. Schaeffer, a bit of an eccentric theologian who warned of the encroachment of secular humanism. He believed that abortion could cause the downward spiral to infanticide and euthanasia. It didn't. He released a series of films called, "Whatever Happened to the Human Race,"[13] depicting abortion with horrific and graphic imagery. The films were pitched to church audiences and the issue of abortion began to motivate Evangelicals, shifting them to the right of the political spectrum. The candidate litmus test was born shortly thereafter.

11. Floyd, "Radical," para 4.
12. Taliesin, "Profile," para 2.
13. Stewart, *Power Worshipers*, 64.

After losing the 1980 election, a Harris poll suggested Carter would have won the popular vote by a margin of one percent if not for the newly minted Moral Majority voting bloc. Falwell said in an interview cited by Politico in 2014, "I knew that we would have some impact on the national elections, but I had no idea that it would be this great."[14] Evangelicals helped to vote Carter into the White House, but four years later turned on him, a fellow Evangelical, to put Reagan in government housing for the next eight years; Reagan enacted the most liberal abortion laws in history as governor of California, just a few years prior.[15]

With all due respect to Aaron Sorkin's HBO series, *The Newsroom*, please indulge me an amended script line, as told by the news anchor, portrayed by Jeff Daniels, "Churchianity is the American Taliban," not the Tea Party, in its seeking to create a theocracy by infiltrating government to bend the GOP leadership's spinelessness to its will. And, although they call themselves "true Americans" and "patriots," their strategy is not uniquely American. Throughout history, authoritarian leaders around the world attempted to consolidate power by co-opting religion through fear.

But wait, there's more. Through worldwide partnerships, including the World Congress of Families, the US based "movement" is focused on a global "Christian Caliphate."[16] The goal is to take down modern democracy and replace it with theocracy. Global liberalism and processes of globalization become the enemy. Science is the enemy. Fear is the drug of choice. Truth be damned. All prayed for in the co-opted name of Jesus.

It is the opinion of this author that Evangelicalism must reimagine its leading brand of American Christianity, free of partisan politics and Bible mismanagement to remain relevant or it will succumb to the trash heap of history. And God will not mind a bit.

Please understand my aim is true, as my faith remains steadfast, but it is simply no longer filtered through the lens of conservatism (or liberalism, lest ye be suspect, which some of you already

14. Balmer, "Real Origins."
15. Stewart, *Power Worshipers*, 67.
16. Stewart, *Power Worshipers*, 43.

are), partisan politics, the "weaponized word," or a manufactured eschatology. All that baggage led to a passive aggressive relationship with the world and a neglected environment that believers are commanded to protect.

It is self-evident to those with eyes to see that Churchianity has embraced a lust for political power over the love of Christ time and time again. Misguided and blind, worshipers crushing on an idolized President Jesus ironically misunderstand and misrepresent the Christ, inasmuch as the first century Jews misunderstood his spiritual ministry in their zeal to procure a political deliverer from Rome.

Since Churchianity co-opted the right wing of the Republican party decades ago, you can clearly distinguish the power surges that led directly to the rise of former President Trump. And now after a historic US Capitol insurrection, leaving in its wake a literal existential threat to American Democracy, a global pandemic, racial tension not seen in a generation, and an ever-looming environmental catastrophe, we are left with a completely impotent, irrelevant, and culpable "church." Astonishingly, "she" has chosen to tow the Republican party line over offering the love of Christ to a nation desperate for authentic good news, leading me to believe "she" is not the church at all.

Over the years, these postmodern pharisees proved to be useful idiots for the GOP, which extorted votes for an agenda bereft of basic Christ-like values, based on the choke hold of the single issue of abortion. While Evangelicals could have used increased influence to press the party to back more Christ-centered positions, instead they either absorbed Republican ideals that have crushed the middle class and poor, or promoted hardline social issues, most of which are at enmity with Christ's teachings of grace, mercy, and love. This jarring discovery led me to believe that the authoritative words of Jesus have little in common with the American branded "Bible-based" religion.

In 2016, anything resembling Jesus was buried in an unmarked grave to propel Trump to the White House. Trump's blatant disregard for the basic tenets of Christianity or basic human decency for that matter were justified and sanctified. In fact, when *Christianity Today* published an article castigating Trump, over two hundred faith leaders doubled down in support of their political messiah.[17]

One single presidential term later, on January 6, 2021, the "fruits of the spirit" decades and centuries in the making were made manifest in a historic, unprecedented act of sedition in an insurrection at the US Capitol. The rioters were overwhelmingly white. And overwhelmingly "Christian."

Without going down the conspiracy-laden rabbit hole, QAnon deserves an annotation. The road to Armageddon and the Second Coming of Christ were paved by date-setter apocalyptic authors who gave a wink and a nod to the brethren that they were not in fact date-setters (See Acts 1:7), but they all believed that the year 2000 was significant, just as the year 1000 was significant to eschatologists a millennia ago. Evangelicals watched with ecstatic anticipation for every nuanced news report about Israel, the EU, and even the Y2K scare, but no return of Jesus in the clouds was in the cards. Then 9/11 happened and twenty years of madness ensued that included a global pandemic, economic catastrophe, wars and rumors of wars, climate change, US sedition, and Trump. Still, no Jesus. No rapture.

Disillusioned, something had to fill the vacuum to propagate dualistic imaginings. QAnon was the perfect mix of good vs. evil, and subsequently damned Democrats to Hell in the process, led by the conspiracist in chief, Trump. In the absence of real leadership and an authentic evolved theology, people will believe anything.

In a bizarre turn of events in an unprecedented pandemic, those beliefs included the mass hallucination that mask mandates were an egregious infringement on civil liberty, but unqualified rebellion is not an American or biblical value. However, acting Christlike in being one's brother's keeper is a value to be held dearly.

Unhinged, lost, fearful, and enraged, many "Evangelical patriots" found themselves in the center of an un-American, antidemocratic mania that could culminate in Civil War 2.0. I have

17. Galli, "Trump," para. 1.

an ounce or two of compassion, limited to a disturbing collective brainwashing, but there are now painful enduring consequences, including the deaths of five people on January 6, 2021, because of blind belief in conspiracies, outright lies, willful ignorance, and Churchianity (See Matt 24:4).

One could argue that there are as many religions, denominations, sects, and cults co-opting the name, if not the teachings of Jesus as there are stars in the Milky Way. One also could and will argue that a dude like me without an advanced theological degree should be immediately disqualified as an authority of the Bible. But in decades of continuous independent study, I am now and forever grateful for exactly that. Further, in chapter three, we will explore how my research led to a self-imposed exile from conservative Evangelicalism to an evolved experiential faith, which blossomed at the time of my mother's death. It is this author's opinion that the weight of experiential faith must gain deeper acceptance and respect to be on par with Scripture and tradition. There are times of miracles and synchronicities that defy explanation and times when words, liturgies, or rituals cannot offer the solace of the peace that passes understanding. Further, what is passing for authority today is overwhelmingly filtered through the lens of decades of religious nationalism, all in the name of revisionist history, in reimagining a Christian nation that never existed.

At the time of this writing, self-appointed "patriots," including a significant population of America's citizenry are hell-bent on a violent overthrow of US democracy in favor of anti-American authoritarianism. At its core: a cult that claims Christ as savior, but Trump as Lord, for now at least. Who and what comes next could be catastrophic to America and the world, as authoritarian leadership is on the march in China, North Korea, Iran, and Russia. All are betting on America's internal distractions in anticipation of America's decline while strategizing major geopolitical moves, except for Russia, now engaging in the annihilation of Ukraine in an egregious act of aggression against a sovereign nation. The free world is stunned, abhorred, and heartbroken by the unprovoked attack that may or may not be the birth pangs of WWIII. This book, however, is built on hope and transformation.

Thus, my faith is not shaken. Hope remains steadfast in the Jesus who lived the example of mercy, grace, compassion, and sacrifice. More truth: what passes as the Christian Right is not the biblical representation of the church at all. They are simply goats who believe they are sheep. I ate my fair share of paper in solidarity for years, so I do not judge, but self-examination is required by all. It is arresting to wake to an understanding that one had not been smart enough to know one had been dumb. I have empathy for all, but that does not mean they should claim authority as Christ's representatives on Earth.

In my heart of hearts, I believe the world is undergoing a paradigm shift in thought and action, wherein Christ transcending all religion, much maligned and misunderstood for two millennia, is transforming the world, while the old guard fitfully struggles to maintain status quo in a last gasp of desperation. My prayer for them is that they will have the opportunity to look at the Gospel with a fresh set of eyes, ears, and unprecedented mindfulness, to come to know Christ intuitively and experientially, and free of duality, which must include the final evisceration of the "us and them" and "good vs. evil" mindset.

Through a wonderous experience beyond space and time, which we will explore in chapter three, I was afforded a glimpse of eternity, to metaphorically see in the dark, which is really what living by faith is all about. It taught me that it is time to know deeper, not more. It is time to unhinge from biased and politically expedient biblical literalism that leads to division, where unity is demanded. Not at the expense of truth, but for the sake of it and an evolved faith wherein the aspiration is to become smart enough to know that we are dumb, to live and breathe in the blessing of the unknowing mysteries of God, the universe, and beyond.

In this evolved faith, experience expands its role in parallel with tradition and Scripture. In this place, death is illusion and simply a seamless transition to life renewed beyond space and time. In this place empathy, grace, mercy, goodwill, mindfulness, wisdom, and justice drive government, business, and science, and in this place love in action is the work of the church.

The subsequent chapters will explore alternative theological interpretations rooted in the ancient faith's wealth of orthodoxy to provide doctrinally credible alternatives for consideration. Through two millennia, Judeo-Christian theological debate has become a rich tradition, inasmuch as Christmas and Easter. This book continues that tradition and may be controversial in certain circles but must be included in the debate. In my experience, it is better to be a man with more questions than answers. In other words, to "be still and know I AM God."[18]

The American church has clearly fallen prey to a false narrative in its belief that somehow through providential oversight God is on our side and is not only American but Republican to boot. The Westernized Jesus is diluted and devolved as a self-absorbed, narcissistic, racist, homophobic, corporate, and political hack, void of grace, mercy, love, empathy, or justice.

Second Chronicles 7:14 is often cited about America's need to repent of its many "liberal-centric" sins, but I contest that an Old Testament Scripture clearly delivered to ancient Israel, and in fact is the "chronicle" of Israel's history, is not transmutable to modern America. Context is everything. Is the Old Testament useful to modern ears? Of course, and we will delve into that topic in another chapter; however, this is one of the more flagrant examples described as Bible mismanagement.

An intuition of God's presence as a young boy lit up a spark inside me. If allowed to blossom, that connection could have vastly improved the disposition of this angry young man's teen angst, indirectly related to my parent's divorce. An intervention by a kind disciple of Jesus could have set my path straight to experience the love of Christ and to see the world through merciful eyes.

Instead, my weed-smoking partner in crime and band mate dropped the Hal Lindsey library in my lap, which I devoured, only to become an end times guru at sixteen. This intellectual understanding of a dispensational eschatology metanarrative became the

18. Ps 46:10, NIV.

core value proposition of my faith. It was absolutely fear-based and at times became an idol unto itself, as I never really experienced the love and peace of Christ personally. Intellectual understanding is not faith, inasmuch as knowledge is not wisdom. Self-loathing for my own hypocrisy waged a war within my soul for decades in a futile attempt to salute this false flag religion. I am convinced this dangerous eschatology is where we derive the aforementioned weaponized word. Still, everything happens for a reason, even if not apparently so. Thus, life's twists and turns led me here. Any other life lived wouldst not this chapter been writ.

This is the backstory to hundreds of thousands of conversions of the last century and beyond. In other words, let's grease the wheels of the apocalypse and to hell with an already condemned world, to hasten the return of the very white, politically expedient Jesus. And through that filter, the lost are to accept this co-opted Jesus as their own customized personal savior through a fear-forward Gospel, meshed with malignant partisan politics at the altar of a perverted nationalism. This is not good news. This is not the Gospel of Christ. This is a cult.

Losing My Religion

LOSING ONE'S IDENTITY OR waking to the reality that one's identity is built on a false narrative is tough to swallow. Many ignore the flashing code red warning signs and choose to live in blissful ignorance. Others choose to blindly follow leaders like lemmings over a cliff. Some will commit to fall on the sword. Most will go AWOL as soon as the sword slices a bit too close to the aorta.

Case in point, during the worst of the pandemic, a storefront sign hanging in a popular Manhattan Mexican restaurant read: "Don't like the mask? You'll hate the ventilator." Many good people followed bad politicians over solid science in disbelief that they were infected with COVID-19 right up until the time they were intubated and begged for the vaccine they willingly refused. It is sad, horrific, and criminal.

I've been there as a recovering fundamentalist. As one who fully embraced the "conservative values" of the Christian Right for over three decades of my life, I can assure you the discovery and realization process is a dreadful experience that hits you at the very core of what you think is your soul. It is in fact, your ego, but let's not go there yet.

Unraveling and untethering from the tentacles of religious nationalism and its ecstatic fever dream–like accoutrements is like a gut punch that knocks the wind out and you just can't catch your breath no matter how hard you try to breathe. It feels quite literally like shell shock long before it feels like emancipation. But trust me, free you will be in time.

"No, I'm really not *that* kind of Christian," the woman at the Wells Fargo bank branch affirmed while trying to underscore her newly discovered nuanced faith stance to a friend in the teller line. In an amalgam of misunderstanding, just what "that" means is difficult to express as a postmodern apologist. It is all a part of the process of recovery and rediscovering who you are in Christ. I contest that there are millions who have lived and died claiming Christ, who never met Jesus, just as there are now millions waking to a new understanding of Christ and trying to express what that "that" means is the key.

Life is easy in the Churchianity ghetto. You are told the who, what, where, when, and why to believe. There is safety in numbers and those numbers include curated chapters and verses cemented into your mind in terms of black and white, right and wrong, left and right, and good and evil, but make no mistake, you are willingly choosing the "blue pill."

Churchianity feels fresh-faced and pure behind the gates of the cozy confines of the community. Yes, the politics and proselytization are merchandized in the front window, but if you're only keen to Monday morning quarterback and don't dig too deep, there are also many lifestyle brands churchianitized for your protection from which to choose. From music to mints, from pillows to chicken nuggets, they are all stamped with the seventh seal of approval and built to both distract from and attract to the juicy center of Churchianity: judgment.

The old song goes, "They will know we are Christians by our love," but the truth is Christians are now widely known as hatemongers. Hatred and intolerance of those deemed sinful in their eyes, the morally bereft, whom they would consider "lost" and in need of salvation are marginalized and judged. All would be friends of

Jesus, to whom his compassion would befall and his love envelope, but to postmodern pharisees, these churchianitists do not have the mind of Christ, so compassion is limited to that of judge, jury, and jailor. And that is what "that" kind of Christian means.

This little book is designed to help clearly define what kind of Christian the woman at the Wells Fargo bank is, not what kind she isn't. I contend that there is only one kind, the others are not Christians at all, yet they move and act with unbridled impunity, imparting judgment on the world. We will explore that which will get me called a heretic by these folks as well as "Trumpangelicals," a more virulent subset of Churchianity in the next few chapters.

Soon after the religious nationalistic spell wore off, I identified as "spiritual, but not religious," but that moniker never truly fit, because throwing out the baby Jesus with the bath water was never the intention. I still believed. My faith was even stronger, yet different. Coming to that realization helped me to finally find the true freedom I believed to have already possessed for decades but was never fully allowed to explore in the ghetto. That freedom provided the courage to research and examine formerly forbidden authors, ancient and modern; faiths, old and new; and my own beliefs, true and false.

There is a fury in mankind that rages at the brevity of life and finality of death. We are here but for a moment and we have work to accomplish. Work that will etch our memory in stone so that future generations will know that we were here. We made a difference. We mattered.

Very few of us have harnessed the spiritual enlightenment of the Dalai Llama, Buddha, or Jesus, but we can and in fact, we are called to that life. Every one of us. No, I am not saying we are all little gods or saying that Jesus did not die and rise as Christ. But the very definition of the word "Christian" means little Christs. All great wisdom masters can simply "be still and know" God is God, we are in God, God is in us, as God is in All, and All are in God. Most of us are far from masters of wisdom. Jesus was such a great master of wisdom, but we relegate him to the suffering servant role as savior of the world and brush his "difficult" and "nuanced" radical, subversive, and awesome teachings aside. Afterall, it's easier that way in the ghetto, right?

If we can squint to see the light of enlightenment in the distance, even for a second, some of that fury will pass. The goal is to live in that space of peace that passes all understanding, so that we can untether from the things of this world, that in the end don't matter one iota.

As a musician, I've always wondered why music is so important to the world. I take great pride as a composer because in my own small way I continue God's creation process by writing musical works. Most are mediocre by human standards, of course, but all were produced from nothing turned into something, and that is the miracle God invented and a gift imparted to us to continue creation.

I had a recent epiphany that led to a new understanding of the importance of music. As we fall deeper in love with a composition, we are absorbed into it as One. I now believe that oneness we feel tucked inside music mimics the oneness we ache for in the midst of our fury. As we are absorbed into the harmony, it replicates how we as eternal spirits are drawn into oneness with God's ultimate love at death's passing. We will dig deeper on this topic in chapter 3, "Life after Death: I Was Told There'd Be Cake." But this is not a morbid book. Death is not to be feared. Full stop. Yet, I am no stranger to that fear. It's a process.

In a dream the other night I was looking out over an abyss below with an expansive panoramic view of the sky before me. A guard rail tethered my life to the ground. As I gazed in wonder at the cosmos, the angel of Churchianity held me close from behind, represented oddly enough by Amy Grant, who also resembled the Ghost of Christmas Past from *Mister Magoo's Christmas Carol*. Full disclosure, I adore Amy Grant and the Ghost of Christmas Past, so no malice is intended. Truth, I swallowed a Benadryl before bed so that may account for the visuals.

The angel said to me, "How does it feel to lose your faith?" I replied, "I do have faith, even greater faith now, and I know that I know because of the aching in my heart that represents my oneness with God. I just have no more faith in you."

3
_____

Life after Death

I Was Told There'd Be Cake

THIS IS THE STORY of an incredibly unique "come to Jesus meeting."
I caught a life changing glimpse of eternity at the moment of my
mother's passing, an extremely rare phenomenon, but other docu-
mented cases exist. If you are curious, and by all means you should
be curious about the reality of *life after . . . life*, please read on.

It has been seven years to the day and hour since my mother
said goodbye to me and life on this planet. It has taken that long to
process exactly what occurred in those brief moments of her passing. However, I knew in the twinkling of an eye those 240 heart-
beats or so were life changing and I would bear the responsibility
to tell the story to the world.

The big question was timing—when to unveil the tale? As I do
not possess that much of a messiah complex, questions persisted if
anyone would care at all. Life, as it turns out, presents moments of
opportunity, say a global pandemic for example.

Hopefully, at the time of this reading, the pandemic is a
distant memory to you. Currently, however, people all over the
world are clamoring for answers, living in isolation, and holding
considerable fear deep inside. A new normal will emerge, defining
this generation. The byproduct of the outbreak is, if nothing else,

a keen awareness that we are all vulnerable beings suddenly forced into a tenuous solidarity. For a minute, at the start of the pandemic there was no "us and them" or numerous granular fractional divisions thereof whether we liked it or not. Now, on the back end of this catastrophe, it is clearly evident that we "like it not," as division is rampant. To vax or not to vax? That is the question. Regardless, we collectively experienced humanity at its basest level of life and death as human constructs and fragile systems of civilization, governance, and culture disintegrated before our eyes. Years into this, humanity is more than frayed at the edges and includes the potential for a US Civil War 2.0 and the actual invasion of sovereign Ukraine by an unhinged and overly isolated authoritarian: Vladimir Putin. How long will this go on? No one currently has the answers. OK God, you've got my attention . . . again.

It was the worst day of my life. Mom was dying. The unresolved issues between us, the success or failure of my start-up, the unmade bed at home, the chaos of life under construction, to be candid, none of it mattered at all now. Death did not graciously stand by and wait for me to get it together. Death, like life . . . happens.

Mom was the perfect amalgam of Elaine Stritch and Jane Fonda. Equally ballsy, courageous, humble, and complex, she led life on her own terms, whether good times or bad, in perfect health or suffering, my mother carried on in modest dignity.

She was a warm and compassionate person, yet she would never say "I love you" unless there was significant potential for impending doom. To be clear, I prayed toward Manhattan on the hour since the day I learned to sing "New York, New York." Any hint of a trip, let alone a move, to NYC would be cause for alarm, triggering the worst in maternal fears. So, like clockwork, before I would hop a train packed with music demos and dreams, she would sheepishly mutter those three little words and I would sheepishly mutter them back, both careful not to look each other directly in the eye. There was usually an added value proposition of discouragement aimed directly at those hopes and dreams, but the entrée of this mother's love always came with a side dish of fear. So it was with Mom.

The Fullness of Love

We did love each other though, which was self-evident. We talked, ridiculously, about five times a day. Most dialogue amounted to work-a-day errand rundowns or current event gossip, but on occasion we could go deep. Philosophical, spiritual, and religious topics consumed us at times and those were the best conversations. Once we even agreed to attempt an otherworldly contact of the other, whoever "went" first. Don't worry, I am not going down that road. This is not about a séance or things that go bump in the night. That's chapter six, so beware.

We spent a lot of time together, mainly in restaurants where she perfected her dead pan line, "This doesn't appeal to me." Mom never blinked once in a stare down with a waiter, as she gingerly pushed both the offending plate and the poor guy toward the edge. She was renowned from Manhattan to San Francisco as a sweet but curmudgeonly "broad" who sent back more food than she ate. The problem for chefs: she was always right, and they knew it. A gourmet (her Thanksgiving feasts would shame Martha Stewart into submission), a food critic, and former restaurateur herself, my mother was the consummate foodie and a very elegant lady. You are getting a pretty clear picture, right?

My all-time favorite birthday cake was, is, and forever shall be banana walnut cake with peanut butter icing, which was her specialty. It is an acquired taste for sure, but to me, it tastes like childhood. The simple mixture of flour, sugar and love was the one thing I dreamed about after the holidays passed in those bleak Mid-Atlantic winters. Headlong into February, it was unfathomable that I would never again watch her inspired bustle in the kitchen, nor would I get to hunker down on a huge chunk of peanut butter heaven next week or ever.

On that day in the ICU, a seismic shift unbalanced our little universe. It was mom's last day on Earth. I will spare you the excruciating details of her illness and the extremely poor choices in medical care she made in those last few years. She did survive cancer twice and added twenty-five years to a life that otherwise would have been snuffed out at forty-nine, save for critical medical interventions. Suffice to say that a perfect storm of health disasters led indirectly to my mother's death, despite the efforts of a team of skilled surgeons, determined resident doctors, and compassionate nurses. Mom was cured of the cancer, but the cure killed her. Three weeks of 'round-the-clock care in overseeing disjointed hospital services, the expectation of full recovery, the heart-breaking setbacks, the look of desperation in my mother's eyes, and the blessed relief of cafeteria breaks were all behind me now.

Mom talked about God like it was a distant signal in space and never believed in organized religion. There was a time when I proselytized, evangelized, and thumped the Bible over her head or anyone that could stand to be near me for more than a few minutes. That was a long time ago. She listened politely, but always found a way to torpedo my efforts. Derisive hits squarely landed on my run at becoming a pastor, believing it to be a phase that would pass like everything else I latched onto for security or distraction. She was correct and I passed on Liberty University. Bullet dodged.

She lived her life with a disdain for the social aspects of church, a trait I shared with her, but in my heart of hearts I believe her protest was more likely driven by insecurity. Mom had a simple, quiet faith of sorts. She kept a Bible. She kept the works of the Dalai Lama. She also kept the works of the Desperate Housewives. All I know is that in my heyday as an AGRO Fundamentalist, more than once she reiterated, "If you want me to have a personal relationship with Jesus Christ, then Jesus Christ let me have it and leave me alone." Words of wisdom.

I managed the courage to watch as the nurse extubated Mom from the contraption keeping her alive. She was given a prescription to "make her comfortable enough to let go more easily." Yes, that smacks of "putting a human down" and was very disturbing, but is commonplace or so I was told. In the end I was grateful. Mega-doses of Xanax and other drugs were pumped into her limp forearm, creating a lethal cocktail that enabled a "passing" in a matter of minutes. My mom fought hard to the end, but this was the end and Xanax would win.

I braced myself for impact, believing emotional disintegration on cue was imminent, because that is what is supposed to happen, right? I had seen it a million times on TV. That is not quite what happened.

All was eerily peaceful as I awkwardly held her hand, finally unshackled of the tangled web of tubes and wires, save for one. The attending nurse was present but perched on the window ledge documenting everything on her laptop. I looked away to the clock on the ICU wall several times. For some reason, I was struck with a compulsion to identify the exact time Mom was going to leave this planet, like I was dropping her off at the departure gate at JFK. But those days were gone. The tiny, almost alien figure barely resembled the robust, larger-than-life powerhouse mom I knew her to be, and she was leaving me for destinations unknown.

I was calm. No, not calm. Numb. And most definitely not in my comfort zone. Then it happened. The final breath. One last tear streaked down my mother's cheek, and it was over.

The natural response would have been to fall on my mother's breast sobbing and screaming out to my Maker. If you knew me, that would never have happened, as I am a bit reserved, truth be told. But "something" intuited to me to step back and look up. I did so, not having a clue as to why.

In that moment, I felt an overwhelming presence of love and peace that I had never experienced before. Love/peace, fused together as one, engulfed my entire being with wave after wave after wave of the tangible, sweet, internalized warm presence of oneness. It felt like the literal fulfillment of 1 Cor 13:12, "For now we see only a reflection as in a mirror; then we shall see face to face. Now I know in part; then I shall know fully, even as I am fully known."[1]

Then it got surreal. I smiled. And smiled some more. In fact, I could not stop smiling and felt very . . . very high. The overwhelming rush of love/peace that possessed me, quite literally, was almost too much to bear. It was a scene beyond reason or understanding and was a literal metaphysical representation of Phil 4:7, "And the peace of God, which surpasses all understanding, will guard your hearts and your minds in Christ Jesus."[2]

---

1. 1 Cor 13:12, NIV.

2. Phil 4:7, NIV.

I asked the nurse, "Did you feel that?" She looked at me quizzically like she missed an earthquake or something. The answer was no. As the event dissipated, I freaked out and asked her if these "symptoms" might have been a stroke or an anxiety attack, but all was well with my body and soul.

I pressed the nurse again, a sweet mature woman in her sixties who had seen it all, asking if she had ever heard of such a thing. She replied, "Well, officially no sweetie, but unofficially yes, your mother's soul passed through you and although a rare experience, I've heard of it occurring. You must've had an extraordinarily strong connection with your mom." My mother's surgeon stepped into the room and remarkably concurred with the nurse. That may have been the greater miracle.

Recently, I met with leaders of a near death experience research organization, the International Association of Near-Death Studies. Dr. Petra Frese, PhD, informed me that my experience is known in their world as an "SDE—Shared Death Experience." It is reportedly extremely rare.

In those few mind-bending moments, I was overcome by a purity of pristine breathtaking love/peace that felt like the very inhabitance of God. There was an absolute presence of mind that what I was experiencing predated humanity. It felt inhuman, but not in the negative connotation we usually associate with that word. The presence was most assuredly spiritual, eternal, and natural at once. I know that sounds strange, but I now believe we will know when it is time to know these things. Any human explanation is nearly impossible, as the "knowing" is designed to be "experienced."

In that moment, both inside space/time and in eternity, I met God wrapped around and inside my mother's spirit as a unitive fusion of love/peace that had physical presence and sensation that could be felt in my soul and spirit and body. In the end, literally and figuratively is where it all comes together, where we utterly understand the concept of oneness, in an infinite unity or an "Infinity" with God, ourselves, and each other.

To me, that metaphysical manifestation was unequivocal proof beyond doubt that there is no death of consciousness, only a transference of energy. To that end, human fear of death must be reimagined as a transformative anticipation, like removing training wheels from your first bike. In that instance, you realize that it is all going to be OK as you speed down the sidewalk and onto a new journey to new frontiers. In the words attributed to John Lennon, "Everything is going to be OK in the end. If it's not OK, it's not the end."

To quote Paul (the other Paul), Heb 11:1 reads: "Now faith is confidence in what we hope for and assurance about what we do not see."[3] But experiential faith, or how we experience God in daily life, whether as rare and dramatic as described here or in the little synchronicities we all experience on occasion, leads to a different read: "Experiential faith is the evidence in what we hope for and the manifestation of what we do not see."

As a collective faith and as humans on this planet, it seems we have lost the ability to intuit or expect these types of interactions with God. Interesting times, however, beget interesting outcomes. These are certainly interesting times.

Part of the problem is an uber-militant dependence on "sola scriptura" or clinging hard to the Bible as the "inerrant" word of God and discounting experience as "just emotion." We will deep dive on this topic in the next chapters. I can assure you what I experienced was not just emotion. It was a physical manifestation of the eternal that burst through to the natural world. Why? Because if there was anyone in this universe that could petition God to punch a hole in a plane of existence to say goodbye to her son, it was my mom.

It seems that love, at times, can manifest superpowers that we cannot readily comprehend. Otherwise, there is no explanation as to why I was chosen to have this stunning and life-changing experience. I was never the guy who sought out the metaphysical on any substantive level nor was I ever into fantasy books or even *Star Wars* for that matter. There is no predilection to the fantastic in me. I do possess a predisposition to intuition and an immersive sense of empathy, but so do many others.

3. Heb 11:1, NIV.

Two millennia ago, the Roman philosopher Cicero queried, "Why do you insist the universe is not a conscious intelligence, when it gives birth to conscious intelligences?" Dr. Robert Lanza, a renegade thinker who was compared to Einstein by *US News & World Report*, has formulated a new "Theory of Everything." His book, *Beyond Biocentrism: Rethinking Time, Space, Consciousness, and the Illusion of Death* is his elegant response to Cicero.[4]

Lanza posits a paradigm shifting theory that consciousness creates the perceived universe, in a reversal of accepted scientific thought that a created universe enabled the development and process of consciousness. Science told us that our universe all began with a Big Bang about 13.8 billion years ago.

Accepted scientific thought states that the universe exists independent of the observer, is made of matter, and is ruled by mechanistic laws like gravity, etc., while consciousness is simply a byproduct. We can observe everything from the farthest reaches of the heavens with a powerful telescope. We can study subatomic particles with sensitive microscopes. And we can reach for a bag of Cheetos in the pantry. Why? Because we perceive an independent physical universe "out there" that has nothing to do with our awareness of it at all.

But as quantum physics and quantum mechanics appeared as credible scientific voices, which support Lanza's theory, those voices claimed that the universe does not seem to exist without an observer perceiving the universe (or the Cheetos). Twentieth-century theoretical physicist John Wheeler similarly stated, "No phenomenon is a real phenomenon until it is an observed phenomenon." Such concepts are new and radical to physics but not to the mind of Cicero or ancient Vedanta Philosophy; Buddhist Scholar Ashwagosha, the seventh-century master, said that there is no existence; we create existence.[5]

To me, Lanza, Wheeler, Cicero, and Ashwagosha are clearly indicating that the mind, not the brain, is the conscious soul, which is integrated with the eternal spirit. Why? Because death is a

4. Faulk, "Biocentrism."
5. Basu-Ray, "Consciousness."

grand illusion—as death cannot exist in a timeless/spaceless world nor can energy die. Past, present, and future are a stubborn illusion because there is no matrix of parallel "nows" or "presents" in our perceived space/time. Thus, everything exists simultaneously but we are limited to experience only in the ever-present "now," while in reality, "all is oneness."

A dead body is quite different from a living one because the "person" has left temporary housing. So a living person is more like an avatar with limited mobility and functionality, yet to be sprung from the mortal coil. Science is required to prove that death is illusion, but personally, the metaphysical experience I encountered at my mom's transition is all the proof I need.

We are all indoctrinated from pre-K to grad school in what is accepted "truth," from religion to science to politics to history, based on the single factor of which time we are born. This little book was created as a disruption to shift the status quo because the equilibrium of civilization is unstable.

My entire being experienced a paradigm shift in belief, philosophy, and purpose in a New York minute when my mom transitioned. Here is what I trust to be true. Mom is alive and transformed in eternal consciousness, all love, all peace, and all Madre. I will simply say thank you to God for punching that hole in time and space, just so a mere mortal like me could be given such an amazing gift. I caught a glimpse of the eternal and was spared the dread of traditionally mourning my mother . . . and just a week before my birthday. But I do miss that cake.

4

The Love Which Moves the
Sun and Other Stars

ONCE UPON AN EVER-PRESENT now, outside of time and space there lived, still lives, and ever shall live a powerful force of love, justice, goodwill, peace, wisdom, and intelligence. Dante described it as, "The Love that Moves the Sun and Other Stars." You might call it "Intelligent Love Beyond the Time/Space Continuum" or the "Universe." Maybe, let's just keep it simple: God.

The truth just might be that God has no name at all. In Exod 3:14, Moses, while on Mount Horeb, asked God to reveal God's name, to which the burning bush replied, "I AM THAT I AM."[1] Father Richard Rohr, in his book *The Naked Now*, posits a beautiful theory that according to Jewish law, Jews are not allowed to utter the name of God. However, the name ascribed that shall not be uttered, "YHWH," could not be uttered as it is intentionally not a name, but our very process of breathing. Thus, any attempt to speak it is "in vain."[2] You cannot utter the name of the Nameless. We all simply breathe in YH, breathe out WH. The sound thereof

1. Exod 3:14, NIV.
2. Rohr, *Naked*, 25.

mimics human breath. Thus, in every breath we take, humanity is praising God for breathing life into our world and our humanity. In our very first and very last breath, all humanity praises God.

This is but one example of what I call Infiunity, the architecture of communal relationship between God and creation in and beyond space and time. On a serendipitous note, focused breathing is the core methodology in the practice of meditation, with all its emotional and physical benefits of well-being. Meditation is a most effective approach to relieve anxiety and ground oneself, yet another synergistic mystery hidden in plain sight for eyes that see and ears that hear. More on that topic later.

The awesome genius of the God of Wonders is inconceivable and beyond human understanding, especially when we capture a fleeting glimpse of an "aha" moment of eternal awareness. Unfortunately, we humans always seem to land on the surface experientially or strangle biblical passages into submission to suit an agenda, only to miss the underlying spiritual message. In this spirit, please open your mind to an alternative approach to the Bible, free of preprogrammed filtration and familiarity of the last century or so.

God operates both within the confines of the universe and beyond in eternity, while simultaneously immersive to our existence in the "natural now" as one experience, requiring no religion or ritual to access. Life flows. Death transforms. If left to propagate without the assistance of religion, existence would amount to a natural flow of experience in communion with God through life on Earth. Simply being immersed in the presence of the Presence would be church. Let's not forget that for thousands of years prior to the written Bible, creation was the first witness to humanity as the incarnation of God. Mankind, however, never quite understood God. The answer lies in the mystery of free will.

Enter religion. As a human construct, religion in many cases amounts to nothing more than an exclusive morality club containing rules of entry and engagement in an attempt to limit experience, protect us all for our own good, and help humanity find the path to God. God requires no path. God simply "is"—as we "are"—all wrapped up together. At best, religion provides a construct symbolizing deep spiritual principles for the uninitiated living in the shallows. As we evolve, however, religious practice will decrease and immersive unitive experience with God will increase. Let us unpack this a bit more.

In the simplest terms, the Bible takes us on a journey wherein God loves humanity through our continued rejection after rejection and failure after failure, but remains steadfast. I would like to call it unconditional love, but cannot, as it is clear by taking the Bible as a whole, in our human understanding, that God's love has evolved, as conditions were clearly spelled out in the Old Testament. It reads as if God is getting to know us little by little and that love grows deeper, more immersive, compassionate, and unconditional in time. True, even in Gen 3:15, Christ is foretold in prophetic terms, but humanity and in particular the Jews had a long row to hoe before the Incarnation.

In Genesis, we see swift, consequential correction in the stories of Adam and Eve and Cain and Abel, culminating with Noah and the seeming destruction in judgement of the known world. Next, God hand-crafted the nation of Israel to lead as an example to the world as to how to live according to God's expectations under the law, which was difficult on the best of days. Israel failed to live up to those expectations again and again, but the Jews atoned for transgression through sacrificial scapegoats, animal sacrifice, and temple practice.

God then sent the Messiah to Israel and subsequently to the world in Jesus, the very essence of God in human form, to teach us how to live and die and live again in solidarity with all humanity. So, God's love evolved to be unconditional in Christ, as the ultimate love is to lay down your own life for another.

However, there is one caveat to interject, which is profound. There is a Romanized Hebraic word *hesed*, which is difficult to translate in English, but let's try this on: "enduring steadfast loving kindness." It is a word that is meant to be experienced as "God's enduring compassion" inasmuch as it must be understood. God's wonderful *hesed* love is from everlasting to everlasting, as declared in Ps 103:17. It is a "steadfast love" that "endures forever."[3]

Hesed love is the very character of God, baked into Hebrew Scriptures as grace-forward laws. Hosea the prophet declared, "I want you to show love, not offer sacrifices. I want you to know me more than I want burnt offerings.[4]

Let's look at the "law of gleaning" as another example. Crops were mindfully planted beyond the borders of farms by the farmers, so the poor could gather it for themselves at harvest (See Lev 19:9–10). Similarly, vineyards and olive groves were not fully harvested to provide for those in need. Graciousness and compassionate courtesies equal *hesed* love.

But the religious leaders in power during the time of Jesus professed and demanded the letter of the law, while neglecting the beautiful spirit of love behind it that Jesus taught, resulting in both the rejection and condemnation of Christ and impossible standards of living for the Jews. Today, we can easily compare first century pharisaic practices to Churchianity. Bluntly, Churchianity is fake good news and fits the description of religion (on a good day) in the earlier paragraph. It is an exclusive morality club, entangled in political conservative nationalism, co-opting the atonement of Christ as a core tenet, but operating from a position of fear and judgment, while missing Christ's profound teachings of grace, mercy, love, hope, and justice.

Jesus rattled accepted thought and religious piety of the time. He taught a radical subversive wisdom and summed up (and fulfilled as the risen Christ) the entirety of the Law and the Prophets, the known Bible of his day, in this paraphrase of Matt 22:37–39: "Love God. Love People." That teaching alone, if allowed to blossom, could have potentially put a lot of people out of work and out of power in the first century (and the twenty-first century, too). It did then and it should again.

He taught that sin meant "missing the mark," the actual translation of the Greek word *hamartia*, which is an archery term. So,

3. Ps 106:1, NIV.
4. Hos 6:6, NLT.

as we go deeper with God, we strive to hit the target, but miss it consistently. We all fall short in transgression, but Jesus did not and does not condemn. He embodies grace, mercy, and redemption.

Further, the word for "repent" in Greek is *metanoia* and literally means to "go beyond the mind."[5] So, when Jesus said, "Repent for the kingdom of God is at hand," or, "The kingdom of God is within you," it could be understood as "to go beyond your mind to enter into communion with God." The kingdom is something you awaken to in life, not die to enter. Repentance is not a get-out-of-hell-free card.

Yes, you will be required to "die" to the self while living an earthly existence, which means to free your ego to empty the self beyond the mind, as Jesus emptied himself of all but love on the cross, which is described as *kenosis*.[6]

Strive to see yourself observing the world and untether from things, from people, from pain, and from constructs to empty your "self" into a place where you find God in communion. This can be done in prayerful meditation, in contemplation of the Word, or simply by pulling yourself into that place as observing the observer in a place of silence and presence. That is another example of Infiunity, which, to be clear, is simply a word I invented to describe difficult, abstract spiritual concepts that would be self-evident today, if enabled to survive as supernatural law in millennia past, as opposed to what went down to suppress them under religious dogmatic rule. We will deep dive on this practice in a later chapter, "The Inner Revolution of Christ."

Christ saved the world through a sacrifice of extraordinary and lavish love in conquering death, the wage of sin. Please understand that in death, as we all die, the sacrifice was a move of divine solidarity with mankind. God loves us through our pain, in us, and as us.

The earliest followers of Christ had a simple faith. They believed Jesus came into the world to teach people how to live and love, performed great miracles of healing, suffered a painful death

5. Bourgeault, "Go Beyond," para. 2.

6. Elwell, *Evangelical Dictionary of Theology*, 651–53.

at the hands of the Jewish and Roman powers, rose from the dead, and ascended to heaven as savior of the world. There were no fractional denominations, no highly developed theological metanarratives, no political entanglements, no self-righteous movements of alienation or exclusive tribalism. The Jesus sect built a community of love, peace, and hope in the first few years after the resurrection, tucked inside a fractional but well developed theological-centric Israel. In fact, even women were highly esteemed in the group, a rarity throughout history. Slaves became as masters and masters became as slaves, all in the name of love. Jesus' teachings flipped the world upside down or more appropriately flipped it back right side up.

To be clear, first-century life under Roman-occupied territory was brutal and brief. Death came early and swiftly. People had no concern for suffering eternal damnation. In fact, hell as we know it was not a part of the lexicon at the time. Concerns were immediate and hyper-focused on food security and survival. A risen Christ that conquered death and promised eternal life? Now, that was intriguing. Jesus offered hope and lasting joy, as opposed to the tenuous and fleeting pursuit of temporal happiness.

To free your mind further, understand that the Jews had the grave to deal with, but no fully developed preoccupation with a preconceived metanarrative of eternal hellfire. *Sheol* was the term used to describe the place of the dead, which has been traditionally represented as hell. Additionally, Rom 6:23 reads, "For the wages of sin is death, but the gift of God is eternal life in Christ Jesus our Lord."[7] So, in taking this information to task in relation to Christ's work on the cross in conquering death, his final statements included three of the most beautiful words ever spoken on Earth, "It is Accomplished."[8]

God relentlessly pursues us all with lavish love, grace, and mercy as we navigate the human experience throughout millennia. Christ conquered death in solidarity with humanity in the resurrection. If the wage of sin is death, Christ saved us from the wages of sin or of missing the mark for all time and all mankind,

7. Rom 6:23, NIV.

8. John 19:30, LSV.

past, present, and future. In his selfless act, we will receive an eternal life of peace in the end.

God's aim is to make grace the highest revelation of glory in creation and eternity (see Eph 1:6). God sent Jesus into creation and made Christ's conquering death on the cross in resurrection the ultimate exhibition of the glory of grace. God's aim is true and does not miss the mark.

However, not everyone is aware of the amazing gift. And not everyone will accept it. But if God's overarching intention is that "all" will be saved, as 1 Tim 2:4 states, "(God), who desires all people to be saved and to come to the knowledge of the truth," then who are we to question God's motives and ultimate authority?[9]

Well, biblical scholars sure feel up to the challenge; they have debated the theory of universal salvation, known as "universal reconciliation," for nearly two thousand years. But, thankfully, from iconic church fathers including Origen, born in the second century, to Father Richard Rohr and Dr. Robin Parry today, notable theologians across the spectrum of Christianity have taken up the challenge. However, what was once widely accepted by many church fathers (including Origen, Jerome, and Gregory of Nyssa) as truth throughout the first five centuries of Christianity, after years of authoritarian power struggles and denominational infighting, competing theories and translations won the battle. Most notably, in Churchianity, universal salvation is anathema. In fact, without the doctrine of hell, most of Evangelicalism would disintegrate, as it is a core tenet of the fear-based religion it represents. Personally, I now believe the entire New Testament foresees universal salvation. Let's just say God has the last word on the subject and leave it there.

Another personal conviction is coming: if you feel the need to condemn someone or a group of people to eternal hell, you have unforgiveness in your own heart and need to give your motives a self-exam. Again, contentious religious beliefs and fear-based proselytizing practices as described earlier must decrease to evolve the faith if it is going to remain relevant and have a meaningful

9. 1 Tim 2:4, NIV.

impact on the world. Every heart that is in Christ must see Christ in all things, in all people, and in all people groups. To quote Jesus in Matt 25:40, "Truly I tell you, whatever you did for one of the least of these brothers and sisters of mine, you did for me."[10] The "least" is whomever I judge as less worthy or more sinful than me in my filthy rags of self-righteousness.

Does a temporary postmortem state of chastisement and purification exist that does not include eternal punitive retribution? Yes, there is room for interpretation, but ultimately "all" are saved to eternal life. This is the Gospel and the promise of salvation, as 1 John 2:2 reads, "He is the atoning sacrifice for our sins, and not only for ours but also for the sins of the whole world."[11]

If you resist God or live a hate-filled life of violence and murder, are the victim of generational abuse, succumb to devastating personal failure, never get to experience who you really are underneath the ego or behind the emotional concrete walls you built to protect yourself, then yes, you may have a more difficult time accepting God's relentless pursuit to love you. But in time you will accept God's love. We all will, as clearly stated in Rom 14:11. It is written: "As surely as I live, says the Lord, 'every knee will bow before me; every tongue will acknowledge God.'"[12] But what if you missed the message? It doesn't matter, refer to that last sentence. Lastly, humanity can intrinsically intuit God's existence throughout creation. To reinforce what was noted earlier, the first incarnation of God manifested exclusively in the natural universe with zero written words or religious constructs.

So, as Jesus summed up the Law and the Prophets of the Old Testament as well as his teachings as simply, "love God, love people," we can additionally sum up the Gospel, the entire focus of the New Testament as, "Jesus died in solidarity with you and rose as Christ to save you from eternal death to awaken into eternal life. No matter what you have done in this life or how guilty you are, and to be clear we are all guilty, you are forgiven." Divine

10. Matt 25:40, NIV.

11. 1 John 2:2, NIV.

12. Rom 14:11, NIV.

forgiveness is not human forgiveness, so let's not pretend we can completely comprehend God who dwells in space/time and in eternity, simultaneously knowing all past, present, and future things. So, in hearing this good news and trusting it to be true is all that is required of you, me, and the whole world.

To seal your confidence, Jesus cried out to God, while suffering on the cross, as stated in Luke 23:34, "Father, forgive them, for they do not know what they are doing."[13] So then, what horrific deed in all human history of man's inhumanity to man cannot be forgiven, if Jesus, Son of the Living God, can forgive those who condemned him to death out of willful ignorance. We are all ignorant and lost. Please also consider supporting texts in 2 Cor 5, 2 Tim, Rom 5, and Titus 3.

What about Hitler? What about Bin Laden? What about Putin? There are no outliers that Christ has not forgiven or cannot forgive. Is there judgement? Yes. All will account for their actions. This is clearly stated by Jesus throughout the Gospels. But if it is also clearly stated that it is God's desire that all are to be saved, then all are to be saved.

What does judgment look like? I believe it will be the opposite of what humanity's dual nature has imagined. And to be clear, yes, the humanity in me says the world would be better if evil incarnations like Putin were removed from the planet to let God sort it all out. But if we are honest, Churchianity would place Anne Frank, who as far as we know died without reciting a "sinner's prayer," in hell alongside Hitler. Is that justice? No.

But when Christ comes face to face with the six million Jews extinguished by Hitler, including Anne Frank, on the day of judgment, his mercy will overcome every one of those precious souls. In turn, Hitler facing Christ in judgment comes face to face with six million Jews who have been forgiven by God for their missing the mark prior to death at the hands of Nazis, thus they will forgive Hitler for his atrocities. Justice starts to look much less human and more divine. Please have a reread of Matt 18:21–35, the parable of the unmerciful servant.

13. Luke 23:34, NIV.

Then Peter came to Jesus and asked, "Lord, how many times shall I forgive my brother or sister who sins against me? Up to seven times?" Jesus answered, "I tell you, not seven times, but seventy-seven times. Therefore, the kingdom of heaven is like a king who wanted to settle accounts with his servants. As he began the settlement, a man who owed him ten thousand bags of gold was brought to him. Since he was not able to pay, the master ordered that he and his wife and his children and all that he had be sold to repay the debt. At this the servant fell on his knees before him. 'Be patient with me,' he begged, 'and I will pay back everything.' The servant's master took pity on him, canceled the debt and let him go. But when that servant went out, he found one of his fellow servants who owed him a hundred silver coins. He grabbed him and began to choke him. 'Pay back what you owe me!' he demanded. His fellow servant fell to his knees and begged him, 'Be patient with me, and I will pay it back.' But he refused. Instead, he went off and had the man thrown into prison until he could pay the debt. When the other servants saw what had happened, they were outraged and went and told their master everything that had happened. Then the master called the servant in. 'You wicked servant,' he said, 'I canceled all that debt of yours because you begged me to. Shouldn't you have had mercy on your fellow servant just as I had on you?' In anger his master handed him over to the jailers to be tortured, until he should pay back all he owed. This is how my heavenly Father will treat each of you unless you forgive your brother or sister from your heart."[14]

Jesus, in Matt 28:16–20, said this, "All authority in heaven and on earth has been given to me. Therefore, go and make disciples of all nations, baptizing them in the name of the Father and of the Son and of the Holy Spirit, and teaching them to obey everything I have commanded you. And surely, I am with you always, to the very end of the age."[15] Note, that he did not tell them to go out and demand a prayer to accept him as a customized personal savior in

14. Matt 18:21–35, NIV.
15. Matt 28:16–20, NIV.

lieu of condemnation to hell. Jesus did not tell the apostles to create a strategic partnership with Rome to build a bureaucratic hegemony to make him an imperial ascended Caesar Christ. He did not tell them to adopt Hellenistic culture or pagan beliefs like hell, the underworld, eternal damnation, or sun-worshiping holidays that would evolve to Christmas. (I am not bashing Christmas. I love it and it is my favorite time of year that is not 75 degrees and sunny.)

Jesus commanded them to make followers in all nations and baptize them. The Greek word in question here is *baptizontes.* The word was widely used in the Greek lexicon for centuries, describing the act of immersing cloth into a dye until the material is totally soaked through the color. Jesus is clearly stating an expectation of a deep, immersive, and meaningful relationship with followers, expert in their ability to love beyond all human reason, as such was/is his teaching. The one thing I have learned in my study is do not accept the obvious literal or metaphorical reading of any Scripture, without stripping your mind, heart, and soul of the prescribed filters you have been programmed to read. Dig deeper. That is where you will find the awesome truths of God.

What would the world look like today if his commandments were executed as described? I believe with my entire being the world would be a much better place to live on Earth, as it is in heaven. As faith evolves, we will get there. Love is the target and why we must strive to hit that mark. I would say all of Christendom has "missed that mark" for two thousand years. If missing the mark is the literal meaning of "sin," well then, what does that say for all of us who claim Christ? Yet, we are forgiven.

How then shall we live in this world? The answer is simple. Love God. Love people. In other words, when we truly act out and love people, accepting them and ourselves for who we are, flaws and all, as we are all flawed, our world, our lives, and our relationship with God will exponentially improve. There will be less strife, greed, stress, war, and hate. Our own selfishness and vices that control us will fall away as we become satisfied and complete in Christ in the fullness of love. Living inside this knowledge and acceptance, while acting out and embodying "grace in action," or loosely translated from the Greek as *charismata*, creates wisdom. Success in life follows wisdom, wherever or whoever we are. This holds true on both micro and macro scales. That is all there is to it. Everything else manifests religion that divides. Love is the answer. It always was and always will be.

Our job on this planet is to shift consciousness from hate to love, without question or pretense. In so doing, Dante's love energy that spins the universe and all things beyond space and time, great and small, expands and elevates positive change and creates a better world, universe, and beyond. Jesus teaches the way to live a transcendent life of detachment of things and people, to be free of all encumbrances and in the ever present now, in love and in Christ.

You will live forever, beyond this temporary existence in a cage of flesh and bone. You are at your core, eternal spirit. There is profound peace and unimaginable love to experience in this world and the next life, which is divinely designed to be a seamless transition from life to life. With specific intention in the spirit of grace, Jesus told a first-century woman caught in an act of missing the mark to "go and sin no more." And that is good news for postmodern man, too.

5

A Novel Approach to End Times

WHAT IF NEARLY EVERYTHING Churchianity believes about the end times is wrong? What if the accepted eschatology metanarrative of the last one hundred plus years fueled self-righteous bigotry, exploited selective sins du jour, imbued apathy toward the defense of the planet's environmental catastrophe, caused wars and rumors of wars, and inflicted more damage than good on an entire generation seeking answers?

In an authentic search for God, many souls despondently, but with good cause, rejected an intolerable allegiance to a conservative nationalist agenda and a mass murdering terrorist Father in Heaven. However, narrow-minded, authoritarian personality types by the millions were drawn to this lower-cased god. If you have ever been side swiped by the drive-by passive aggressive slam, "Bless your heart," you know who I am talking about. I am waxing poetic of course, but overall, in my experience, Churchianity talks a good game of grace, but walks the path of judge, jury, and jailor. I was one of them.

Now and forever, this book will be labeled "heresy" by the far right "agro-fundamentalists," but that is fine by me. Either God is big enough to ask the tough questions or God is not God. In fact,

God may appreciate a good wrestle. "Jacob wrestled an angel and the angel was overcome" is more than a line from a classic U2 song (See Gen 32:22–30).

I have been on a search for the ultimate truth since childhood. You might be inclined to say that is an admirable pursuit, but any "woke" nugget was merely an intellectual win. It did nothing to build a robust experiential life of peace. In fact, it left me emptier. So, as we endeavor a new road together, understand that I am presenting this alternative to the generally accepted Evangelical Hollywood ending of the world only to show you that there is actual freedom in unknowing such things. Sometimes referred to as the "Cloud of Unknowing," the theme of which dates to AD 398 in St. Augustine's "Confessions," it can provide that "peace that passes understanding" described in the Bible. And you know you want it. We all want it. You do not need to understand the deep intricacies of God's mystery to simply experience God's love. Full stop. With that as our baseline entry point, come, let us reason together.

I am just going to rip off the band-aid to bluntly state that the much maligned, misunderstood, and mishandled Book of Revelation is absolutely a beautiful and befitting climax to the Bible, but it is not a secret decoder of prophecy. It is, however, a love letter of encouragement by an exiled pastor, writing to his congregation under threat of annihilation by the Roman emperor, Domitian.

To post–first century readers, the Book of Revelation reads more like *Game of Thrones* on acid. There are beasts and harlots and horned creatures with dozens of eyeballs looking and watching and fighting and worshiping on Earth as it is in heaven. It is a lot to take in. The recipients of the letter, however, completely understood the narrative because the author was speaking their language culturally, in the context of contemporary understanding of current events in the city of Ephesus and the greater Roman Empire in an "apocalyptic" style. Thus, it is imperative that we understand the background to have any semblance of an immersive comprehension of difficult text. Be prepared for some eye-widening revelations. Pun intended. I apologize in advance for all of them.

As if the vast Greco-Roman pantheon of gods was not enough, the Roman emperors, or Caesars, also demanded worship as gods, and not just any gods. They each set themselves up as God with a capital G.

> Great are You our Lord and God
> Worthy are You to receive honor
> And power and glory
> Worthy are You Lord of the Earth
> To inherit the kingdom
> Lord of Lord, Highest of the High
> Lord of the Earth, God of all things
> Lord God and Savior to Eternity.[1]

No, that is not a new worship hit by Michael W. Smith. That is a song of praise to Domitian, sung by twenty-four elders, all dressed in white and crowns of gold.[2] Now, peek at Rev 4:4 for your first of several holy-smokes moments. Emperor worship was vastly accepted and widely practiced. Let's dig in.

Just prior to the start of the first century, poets including Virgil, extra-biblical prophets, and astrologers, all divined through signs in the skies that "someone" was coming into the world to shift the human condition in a mediation of heaven and Earth. Two millennia later we know that "someone" was most definitely Jesus. There is no credible historian today who does not believe a human being named Jesus walked the planet in the first century, which is also why the first century is called "the first century."

A popular phrase of the time, "Are you the One who is to come?" may have been directed at Jesus by the Pharisees, but was most definitely directed at Julius Caesar, the Roman emperor, who proclaimed himself as the Eternal God of the Universe. Subsequently, his son, Augustus, was called "Son of God." Poetry of the time included the line, "I saw the Son of God ascend to the right hand of the Father," referring to Julius and Augustus. Coins were minted with the inscription, "There is no name save Augustus, by

---

1. Bell, "Revelation," in Patterson, "Rob Bell."
2. Bell, "Revelation," in Patterson, "Rob Bell."

which man can be saved."[3] Every emperor to ascend to the throne thereafter augmented their own "god" story to suit whatever narcissistic or politically expedient needs were required to dominate, intimidate, and subjugate the masses. All these phrases are found in one form or another in biblical text relating to Christ, which also proves just how subversive, remarkable, and dangerous the teachings of Jesus and his disciples were and are now.

Ephesus was a cosmopolitan world trade center and gateway to Asia with its fine silks and spices, which affluent Roman citizens found luxurious. The Agorre was a marketplace where international trade was conducted daily. To buy or sell, each merchant and consumer was required to offer incense to Caesar. It is believed that an ink mark on the hand offered proof of allegiance. This posed a problem for early Christ followers, who identified Caesar and Rome as antichrist, commonly referred to as the "Beast."[4] So, the earliest Christians were fraught with a decision to either eat and take the "Mark of the Beast" or starve and follow Christ. Yes, that does sound like the premise of every end-times movie starring Kirk Cameron. No child star was left behind in writing this chapter.

Before we deep dive on the tyrannical Domitian, it should be noted that upon the suicide of Nero (ruled 54–68 AD), four emperors took the throne within one year including Vespasian, who finally stabilized and restored Rome after a near fatal wound of its power. Does this sound familiar? Please refer to Rev 13:33 and 17:8–12. Again, understanding the background and to whom a work is addressed can turn on the lights for readers today.

Domitian, son of Vespasian, demanded to be called, "My Lord and My God", even by his own wife, Domitia. "Shockingly," she had a hand in orchestrating Domitian's murder in his own home at just forty-five years old.[5] All commissioned statues were required to be made of solid gold and inscribed, "Son of God, Our Salvation," and

---

3. Bell, "Revelation," in Patterson, "Rob Bell."

4. Bell, *Jesus Wants*, 132.

5. Tranquillus, *Lives of the Twelve Caesars*, 8.

he began all letters to be used by procurators with, "Our Lord and God commands."[6]

Domitian had his own brand of "special" Olympic games. It is no secret they were blood baths, of course, but the following should be noted when studying the Book of Revelation. Notably, a masked "cleaner" masquerading as Hades, the god of death and the underworld would sweep the dead bodies from the stage.[7] Both Hades and Death are described in Revelation as being thrown into a Lake of Fire in judgement.

Next, as a ceremonial opening to the games, the leaders of the various provinces were paraded in front of Domitian, where he would both compliment and admonish each of them. He would ramble off things like "I hold this against you" and "I know your deeds."[8] Now compare Revelation, beginning in chapter 2, wherein John addresses various churches in Asia Minor with the exact approach. Oh, and four horses of different colors battled in the Domitian Games, which is remarkably like the four horsemen of the apocalypse described in Revelation.[9]

Every year on Domitian's birthday, he would travel to Ephesus, the world headquarters of Domitian worship, which could be described as a megachurch for the criminally insane. As travelers approached the port from any direction, a 27-foot-tall statue of Caesar Domitian dominated the skyline, which stood atop a platform subjugating subordinate statues of prominent Greco-Roman gods just in case a sojourner had any bright ideas of insurrection. Significantly, the statue held a scroll in its hand. But who was truly worthy to open that scroll? Revelation 5 clearly states that it is not Domitian, but the precious Lamb of God, who is the risen Christ.

Altars were set up throughout the city for the birthday boy, for groups of craftsmen, merchants, and artisans to offer allegiance in worship of Domitian as God. Refusal resulted in instant death.[10]

6. Tranquillus, *Lives of the Twelve Caesars*, 8.

7. Bell, "Revelation," in Patterson, "Rob Bell."

8. Bell, "Revelation," in Patterson, "Rob Bell."

9. Bell, "Revelation," in Patterson, "Rob Bell."

10. Bell, *Jesus Wants*, 32.

There was a Christian group known as the Nicolatians, who proffered that as followers of Christ, it was cool for them to offer fake praise to Domitian, as he was just a narcissistic politician. Why? Because they had families to feed and lives to live. But to the larger Christ following community, worshiping Domitian was an apocalyptic problem. No pun intended.

John, the exiled leader of the churches in Asia Minor and author of Revelation, was woefully aware of the issue. As a caring pastor, he wrote a letter to his flock to encourage them to remain steadfast as a testament of faith to the world, in the face of annihilation. I will not deny that John had a genuine metaphysical vision, but regardless he used wild imagery and metaphor to describe current events intimately known to his audience.[11] Voila, may I present the Book of Revelation.

Let us take a moment to reflect on the courageous and faithful unto death, earliest of Christ followers who suffered under Domitian. Please, now read the first five chapters of Revelation considering the above new information and without pre-programmed filters.

OK, so then you might be asking, what about all the other biblical references describing the "end of days" or the "fullness of time" or "last days"? I never imagined in my wildest dreams that I would be suggesting the following to be true in light of my history with Hal Lindsey books in my teens, but I'm going to come out and say it. The Bible is quite clear and direct and points to 70 AD at the destruction of the Jewish Temple and Jerusalem by Rome.

That equivalent to the nuclear bomb dropped on Hiroshima was absolutely the apocalypse to the recipients of the original Scriptures, Epistles, and Gospels. The writings were not intended for twenty-first century doomsday groupies or wannabe novelists. Yes, the Bible offers powerful spiritual and moral teachings to us today, but again context is everything.

The time period between the birth of Jesus and the destruction of the temple in 70 AD were the end times, but particularly from the date of the time of crucifixion thereon, as temple worship

11. Bell, *Jesus Wants*, 32.

was no longer accepted by God. Worthy of note is Matt 27:50–51, which reads, "And when Jesus had cried out again in a loud voice, he gave up his spirit. At that moment, the curtain of the temple was torn in two from top to bottom."[12] The temple curtain separated the Holy of Holies (the most revered section of the temple) from lesser holy sections. The tearing of the curtain signified the end of the temple-centric covenant as humanity entered a new covenant with God through Christ.

God meant business in the redemption of humanity. The Jewish Messiah did not die in solidarity with humanity to conquer death, the wage of sin, to allow the continued temple worship practices of the splintered legalistic sects that Judaism devolved to in those times. Rome, through divine appointment, prophesied in Scripture and spoken of by Jesus in Matt 24, destroyed the temple, leaving "not one stone upon another" and delivered the remaining Jewish population to the Diaspora, all in the time and space of his generation, which "did not pass away." Prophecy fulfilled. But fundamentalist teachers subjugate the prophecy to their will, claiming that the teaching is a prophecy yet to be fulfilled, so that "generation" is translated at times as a "race" of people that sees these things come to pass, so in other words, "that race of people would not pass away before seeing these things come to pass." But clearly "these things" were hyper focused on the destruction of the temple, regardless of mentions of earthquakes and assorted apocalyptic telegraphing.

That leads us to the formation of modern Israel in 1948, which is central to modern end-times metanarratives. Fundamentalist eschatology baked in the notion that the generation alive in 1948 would live to see Jesus return in the clouds. A biblical generation was thought to be forty years, so all eyes were on 1988-ish. No Jesus. End times teachers kept expanding on the definition of what "generation" meant. Was it forty years? Fifty years? Well, here we are nearly a quarter into the twenty-first century. No Jesus. But the fundamentalist's fundamental flaw is that modern Israel is not under the Old Testament biblical covenant. It does not follow any of the terms of obligation of that covenant. For example, the

12. Matt 27:50–51, NIV.

Jews were forbidden to fund or maintain a vast military, stockpile weapons, make foreign alliances, or conscript a man into service, to be completely dependent on God for protection. The prophets considered militarization a form of idolatry, which was a blatant violation of Israel's covenant with God (see Deut 20 and Mic 5). That is not modern Israel by any means.

John the Baptist, the itinerant Jewish apocalyptic preacher, forewarned that the end was near. He was the forerunner to Jesus preparing the nation of Israel for the Messiah. In fact, Jesus launched his ministry to the world on the banks of the Jordan, in a water baptism by John. Jesus came as a healing balm to bring inner peace in Christ to the Jews in preparing them for a world without a temple or a nation of Israel and forewarned that the end was near. It was. And it all happened forty years later in 70 AD at the destruction of the temple and the resulting Diaspora of the Jewish population around the world, and that generation did not pass away before the end came.

Let us look at Isa 2:2 that reads, "And it shall come to pass in the last days, that the mountain of the Lord's house shall be established in the top of the mountains and shall be exalted above the hills; and all nations shall flow unto it."[13] This was a promise tucked inside a prophecy of the coming kingdom, fulfilled in the first century at the time of the New Covenant and cemented at the destruction of the temple with brutal finality. Christ is the new temple, and all nations of people flow in, out, and through him in the ever-present now. In Matt 28:20, Jesus states, "And surely I am with you always, to the very end of the age."[14]

When is the end of time? Paul tells the Corinthians to listen up and reveals hidden things.

> Behold, I tell you a mystery: We shall not all sleep, but we shall all be changed—in a moment, in the twinkling of an eye, at the last trumpet. For the trumpet will sound, and the dead will be raised incorruptible, and we shall be changed. For this corruptible must put on incorruption,

13. Isa 2:2, NIV.
14. Matt 28:20, NIV.

and this mortal must put on immortality. So, when this corruptible has put on incorruption, and this mortal has put on immortality, then shall be brought to pass the saying that is written:

"Death is swallowed up in victory.

O Death, where is your sting?

O Hades, where is your victory?"

The sting of death is sin, and the strength of sin is the law. But thanks be to God, who gives us the victory through our Lord Jesus Christ.

Therefore, my beloved brethren, be steadfast, immovable, always abounding in the work of the Lord, knowing that your labor is not in vain in the Lord.[15]

The word "last" (last trumpet in verse 52) or "*eschate*" in the Greek, means "the extreme end." Yes, there will be a second coming of Christ where those alive on that mystery day will be transformed in the blink of an eye shedding the weight of the material world to become glorified in a spiritual, incorruptible body without tasting death. And we will be in God and God will be in us and God will be All in All as One.

Someday God will say "Enough!" and that will be that. It might be 300,000 years from now or the very next blink of your eye. For now, we have work to do, "to be steadfast, immovable, always abounding in the work of the Lord." Full stop. Translation: we can no longer ignore our responsibility to be good stewards of the planet or shove the world into self-destruct mode in hopes of a get-out-of-tribulation-free card. So, let it be the end of the end of the world as we know it, and feel fine about it. And in so doing, "them" of "us and them" fame, suddenly look more like our brothers and sisters, not the enemy to judge.

My end-times research included the work of Roman historian Suetonius and was in part inspired by a video sermon and conversation with Rob Bell.[16] None of the teachings in this chapter are new revelations or a new orthodoxy. Many Christians believed these teachings two thousand years ago and continue to do so today.

15. 1 Cor 15: 51–58, NIV

16. Bell, "Revelation," in Patterson, "Rob Bell."

6

Hell Is Too Big to Fail?

CUE THE SCARY MUSIC. No, seriously. Believe it or not, I came face to face with a ghoulish, scary as all literal hell demon who attempted to murder little old me. Thanks to the grace of God, I was able to "perform" an exorcism of sorts on a seriously deranged man one dark and stormy night at midnight in Manhattan, no less. And not just any man; Clark was to be the best man at my wedding only a few years later. This is a true story.

I was introduced to Clark, our friendly neighborhood Satanist drug dealer, by a former girlfriend, Jaynie, who wanted to buy some pot, as one does at seventeen. He invited us into his lair, and we got into a deep philosophical chat, which was always enticing. The pot, not so much, as it made me more anxious than chilled out, so any delay of an illegal, panic attack–inducing purchase was fine by me.

Ten minutes in, he had already regaled us with tales of demon-conjuring adventures. He was clearly in over his head and sadly out of his mind because little devils apparently and quite regularly dropped by his studio apartment on Delancey Street. Clark advised that a snickering dwarf-sized demon lurked behind me at that very moment with ill intent. We split posthaste and managed to avoid Clark for a year. The weed was good. No panic attack.

Then, while strolling hand in hand on a tree-lined courtyard path strewn with smashed liquor bottles, used condoms, and drained heroin syringes, we came face to face with Clark again. He was distributing Bible tracts to junkies in Tompkins Square Park and was genuinely overjoyed to see us, as he sermonized tirelessly about how we too could be "saved by the blood of Jesus Christ, re-born, and baptized in the Holy Spirit." Clark was now born-again. This was intriguing.

A very charismatic guy, both in personality and in denomi-national preference, he had a kind of Harrison Ford meets Jack Nicholson circa *The Shining* vibe complete with an ever-present three-day beard stubble. An imposing figure at 6 feet, 6 inches, Clark was actually a very gentle but lonely and deeply troubled soul.

Jaynie and I were enamored with his about-face and decided to attend church with him on a whim. We became pals. He im-mediately proceeded to "deliver" me from demonic oppression on a daily basis. Apparently, I had a lot of demons living inside me, being a musician and all. In parallel, I was baptized in a Holy Spirit many, many times who apparently demanded evidence thereof in the speaking of tongues. Neither demon nor utterance of ancient Sanskrit drooled past my lips, but I did accept Christ as my per-sonal customized savior for the nineteenth time in about nineteen months, starting with a "prayer with Pat" on the 700 Club.

As noted, one dark and stormy night, literally, I am not mak-ing this up, Clark crashed in my Lower East Side apartment. Al-phabet City 1985 BG (Before Gentrification) was a rough couple of blocks. It might sound crazy to readers under twenty-five but get-ting a cab—after dark—in a snowstorm—in my neighborhood was unheard-of back then. Cops avoided Alphabet City like it was Kan-dahar on the Hudson. Now, there is a Starbucks on every corner.

Around the stroke of midnight, I was engrossed in an episode of SNL. Clark was deep into the Ryrie Study Bible, locked on the page about Satan's attributes, as of course he was. He was perched about five feet from me staring into oblivion when I noted his head spiral in typical horror movie fashion, pivoting in my direction. I laughed guardedly at Clark, as of course I did, many, many times before. He questioned my faith in the Holy Spirit, saying, "Eric, how strong is your faith in the Holy Spirit?" in a gravelly, but very much Harrison Ford meets Jack Nicholson voice. I replied, "Umm, pretty good?"

In the twinkling of an eye, he had me pinned against the wall. His Hulk-like fists choked my neck. He shouted blasphemies, assorted obscenities, and threatened to kill me, which was evident by the fact that he was attempting to do exactly that. I had to convince myself this was really happening.

In my mind's eye, I envisioned gold sparkly dust flakes flowing in and around me. I remember feeling a deep peace in the face of such violence, but nothing like the shared death experience described at my mother's passing. I recall incanting words that I've never said or read before in my life: "I cast you to dark, dry desolate places in Jesus' name!" He fell to the floor shivering. I was shivering as well, but the room never lost temperature like in *The Exorcist*. It was sheer adrenaline and terror. I told him to get the hell out of my apartment, but he shriveled into the fetal position and would not budge. I fled the apartment, raced down the street to Jaynie's loft and slept outside her parents' bedroom door. When we all ventured back in the morning, my apartment door was wide open. Clark was gone.

Fast forward seven years. I ran into the demoniac again; he was now missing a few teeth, but married with a child. I was engaged and about to get married (not to Jaynie). He asked for forgiveness and insinuated that his possession drama might have been staged, but never truly confessed to the deed. We cautiously rekindled our friendship and for a few months he seemed stable-esque. I reluctantly asked him to serve as best man because my closest pal spent the last three months off the coast of Alaska on a fishing boat and missed his flight back to NYC. The wedding day went off without a hitch or hint of demonic activity, so all appeared well with his soul.

We lost touch again shortly thereafter, but from time to time I would hear bits and pieces of his life from former church mates that he was off the rails. He suffered bouts of major depression, had trouble holding down work, and was now divorced. I never saw him again. A few years later he dove off a fifty-foot quarry cliff into shallow water and was killed instantly when his skull collided with riverbed rocks.

I will never know in this life if the perceived events of that stormy night were a collective psychosis, imagined, real, or a combination thereof. Whether a demon was present or not, I surmise no. However, God was present as I was protected in a remarkable way from a most dark deed, at least I think so. Technically, I did cast out a demon in theory, in the spirit of the circumstances. Was Clark so mentally ill, that even in his psychotic break he simply bought into the understanding that a disciple of Christ could cast out demons? Did I hear those bizarre words I uttered in a film years before? Maybe. It was a very harrowing experience that left an indelible mark on my soul to this day.

Here is what I know to be true. Clark was a Satanist turned born-again Christian. He lived for fantasy because his reality was too painful to deal with and would have exposed him as insecure, unworthy, and less of the macho man he paraded around as his ego. It seemed no matter which side he was on, the fantastical other world magnetized him. He was a sweet guy and I miss him.[1]

As of 2017, about 35 percent of non-Evangelical born-again Christians believe in the existence of Satan, according to the latest Barna Group research.[2] Most Evangelicals would find that statistic troubling, as 98 percent of them believe Satan is a real living being,[3] but I find it refreshing and positive. More disturbing, it seems our collective basic understanding of Beelzebub is an amalgam comprised of medieval literature, religious tradition, and

1. Names and scenarios were changed in my personal encounter story to protect the privacy of individuals and families, but the tale is 100 percent true.

2. Barna, "How We Got Here," para. 14.

3. Barna, "How We Got Here," para. 8

cultural perception created in, wait for it . . . Hollywood. Ladies and gentlemen, may I present, "America."

But the Bible clearly states that Jesus regularly cast out demons, some of whom knew his name and position as Christ. I am inclined to believe those are allegorical stories, particularly Mark 5:1–20 as follows:

> They came to the other side of the sea, to the country of the Gerasenes. And when he had come out of the boat, there met him out of the tombs a man with an unclean spirit who lived among the tombs; and no one could bind him anymore, even with a chain; for he had often been bound with fetters and chains, but the chains he wrenched apart, and the fetters he broke in pieces; and no one had the strength to subdue him. Night and day among the tombs and on the mountains he was always crying out, and bruising himself with stones. And when he saw Jesus from afar, he ran and worshiped him; and crying out with a loud voice, he said, "What have you to do with me Jesus, Son of the Most High God? I adjure you by God, do not torment me." For he had said to him, "Come out of the man, you unclean spirit." And Jesus asked him, 'What is your name?" He replied, "My name is Legion; for we are many." And he begged him eagerly, not to send them out of the country. Now a great herd of swine was feeding there on the hillside; and they begged him "Send us to the swine, let us enter them." So, he gave them leave. And the unclean spirits came out, and entered the swine; and the herd, numbering about two thousand, rushed down the steep bank into the sea, and were drowned in the sea. The herdsmen fled and told it in the city and in the country. And people came to see what it was that had happened. And they came to Jesus, and saw the demoniac sitting there, clothed and in his right mind, the man who had had the legion; and they were afraid. And those who had seen it told what had happened to the demoniac and to the swine. And they began to beg Jesus to depart from their neighborhood. And as he was getting into the boat, the man who had been possessed with demons begged him that he might

be with him. But he refused, and said to him, "Go home to your friends, and tell them how much the Lord has done for you, and how he has had mercy on you." And he went away and began to proclaim in the Decapolis how much Jesus had done for him; and all men marveled.[4]

First note that Gerasenes was a Greek-influenced Gentile settlement. Secondly, the narrative follows a heavy parable section in Mark. Finally, the terminology associated with demons evolved through the ages from the Platonic Greek era meaning "lesser gods" but later in the Christian era became known as demons under the influence of Satan. To elaborate, Syracuse University's Dr. Ken Frieden wrote:

> The exorcism story does not merely recount an event but bears myriad potential meanings. It suggests the effort of Christianity to drive out foreign, especially pagan influences, epitomized by the multiple "*daimones*" (originally lesser Greek gods, later demons) that had become unacceptable to a nascent monotheistic system. As represented in the gospels, Jesus reasserts the unity of God by showing that other supposed deities are merely evil demons. In the course of his travels, he shows his ability to rid Palestine of its evil demons and its competing polytheistic systems; he dispenses with the long Greek tradition that spoke of *daimones* in positive terms. Furthermore, the story of his successful exorcism might be understood as an indirect political statement. We know that Roman legions were prominent in first-century Palestine, and that there were numerous rebellions by the local population, ultimately leading to the destruction of the Second Temple in Jerusalem. Since the demoniac says his name is "Legion," this could suggest a disguised, subversive meaning: as Jesus drives out a legion of demons into the swine, so his contemporaries might rely on him to drive out the Tenth Legion of Roman conquerors. His views are sometimes more explicit, as when he proclaims: "Render to Caesar the things that are Caesar's, and to God the things that are God's" (Mark

---

4. Mark 5:1–20, NIV.

12:17). Although we can read the Greek gospels in any number of more or less scholarly English editions, the problems of translation are not so readily solved. The meaning of this text frequently depends on its precise attempt to reappropriate and transform Judaic and Hellenistic thought. No English rendition can retain the exact verbal components that embody this textual revolution. From a modern point of view, we might be inclined to see the demoniac as a man suffering from psychosis. Yet ancient authors seldom believed that such disorders could be explained as purely individual conditions. Instead, they assumed that the disturbances were caused by the intervention of supernatural beings.[5]

The Bible is humanity's story of God's communion with man, as inspired by God. It is not the "inerrant" word of God, at least inasmuch as Evangelical fundamentalists would have you believe. Second Timothy 3:16 reads, "All Scripture is inspired by God and is useful for teaching, rebuking, correcting, and training in righteousness," but inspiration is one thing, interpretation is another.[6] Scripture has been misunderstood and misrepresented to justify violence, war, racism, false doctrine, and crimes of all kinds. It could be argued that it is the most dangerous book in history. I will argue that it tells the story of God's evolving yet steadfast and enduring love for mankind over thousands of years. If we immerse ourselves at the macro level of resulting outcomes of coalescing Bible narratives, then certain confusing micro level story lines and presumed discrepancies described therein will make more sense contextually. That is our goal and sets us on the right track of an evolved faith.

Most people just do not get this concept. So, religions developed to help structure some semblance of understanding and distill basic core rules and regulations, but in the end religion stifles and constricts. The Spirit of God does the exact opposite in that it frees a soul to experience oneness mindfully both internally and externally, as the Christ disciple sees Christ in all things and all people.

5. Frieden, "Language of Demonic," 49.

6. 2 Tim 3:16, NIV.

God does not require a Bible, an interpretation thereof, a religion, a building, or a complex systematic theology to communicate and connect with a human being. God "is" as we "are" and interconnected as One. As Jesus said on the cross, "It is accomplished." He is the new temple. If we open ourselves to experience, we can see God in creation and in our lives through love and caring for each other.

But free will is a tricky little thing and can also add to our confusion when we do not feel God acting on our behalf in times of great agony. If you can open your mind to the concept, it is self-evident and surely explains why God appears to be in absentia during holocausts, pandemics, and wars.

Let's macro free will out a bit. Where was God when the church became a corrupt theocracy in the Dark Ages? Where was God when the crusades slaughtered thousands in the name of "Christ"? Where was God on 9/11 or now in Ukraine? Where is God today as countless pedophile priests rape little boys? Where is God today while televangelists financially and spiritually rape the faithful? Where is God when the other team wins? Not to sound flippant, but it does not matter because Jesus said, "It is accomplished." Free will at a macro level can easily be misinterpreted as: God hates us, is dead, does not care, or never existed.

Now, let's micro free will in a bit. Imagine an adult who suffered sexual abuse as a child. The person's entire life was shaped by those experiences and built out a worldview that began and ended in objectifying women and/or men, accompanied by an unhealthy emotional outlook causing anxiety to the extent where precious moments of life are missed, and key benchmarks of growth are diminished. This person may also act out sexual abuse on a family member or neighbor and not understand why or have the capacity to understand any of it. This person is dubbed a "lost sinner." If this person does not accept Jesus as his/her personal customized savior, it means "curtains" in hell.

Now, let us imagine this same person is a girl of thirteen and dies unexpectedly in "sin," struck by a school bus. She never accepted Christ as her personal savior. Is she in hell? Fundamentalists will say yes. Why? There is a subjective "age of accountability" found nowhere in the Bible, used as a barometer of adulthood. More than likely, it parallels the Jewish Bar/Bat Mitzvah at thirteen, because of course by thirteen every human on earth has acquired the knowledge of good and evil and has sinned, right? Further, in America, the Gospel is fully accessible and available to all 24/7 on all devices and in the pulpit of countless churches. So of course this girl would have rejected the Gospel, if not saved already, and deserved to be in hell, right?

Let's go further down the rabbit hole to ask additional questions. Which Gospel did this unfortunate girl hear? Which denomination preached it? If it was a "progressive liberal church" did it count? What if the Gospel she heard was preached by the hate-fueled Westboro Baptist Church? What if she was questioning her sexuality and was brainwashed to feel evil incarnate because of it and subsequently unworthy to accept Christ, believing she had to change first for God to find worthiness? It does not matter. "It is accomplished," Jesus said so. It all boils down to this: the dramatic complex web that makes up a human life cannot be inserted into a machine constructed of dogma, ritual, or interpretative subjective Scripture to magically pop out a singularity of salvation.

We live on a wild, beautiful mess of a planet filled with flawed humans in a world where the course of human events is altered by corrupted DNA "files," an unpredictable environment and a world we barely understand. The universe is ordered and logical, albeit we humans, the "free radicals," wreak havoc and run amok, causing the world to appear random and illogical. So, our dualistic mind seeks out a way to define it all and voila: the devil made me do it and a god can make me right, but only if I say the magic words in the prescribed days of my life in the right church to the right god.

There is real suffering in this world. God aligns with humanity individually and corporately in solidarity in the suffering and death of Jesus the Christ, who was, is, and always shall be the Living Logos (Word, in Greek). Long before the written word was, Christ is. Long after the written word disintegrates in dust, Christ is.

Also, please do not discount the agony and horror of death itself. The wage of sin is death, which Christ conquered on the cross. That fact does not make it any easier on any given day of the week for anyone dying or in mourning, particularly today. A global pandemic shut down 2020 and 2021, and the world continues to reel from it. Where is God?

The devil did not create the virus. God did not curse humanity with the virus. What caused the virus? Free radical humans running amok eating "delicacies" that should not be consumed in the first place from an unsanitary wet market in China. Well, maybe, the jury is out on the origin, but it was not a plague sent by God . . . or the "gays." It may have been a tragic Chinese lab accident or worse or simply a naturally developed bug. Time will tell.

As humanity consistently chooses to create hell on Earth every day through free will, that torment is compounded with the agony of death individually and corporately. Free will means that God lets us choose our own paths. Scaled up and out, it can appear as though God does not care about holocausts, pandemics, or insert the catastrophe du jour here. Free will also dictates that there must be an option to say no to God. Living and dying and living again eternally void of God's love would be a hell unto itself, as at times life on Earth is, too. But, as Jesus accomplished the task of salvation, we are made complete and whole in Christ. All humanity can experience oneness with God, in time. Or better to say, outside of time.

Personally, I am agnostic as to the existence of Satan. I will not give credence to any belief that it has a personhood or power equal to God, or remotely close. Way too many people of faith give Satan way too much power and see a devil behind every rock in fear or use it as a scapegoat for individual or corporate sin. To be clear, humanity's free will engine is more than qualified to commit atrocities in macro and microbursts without bringing a more than likely mythical creature into the mix. A global collective conscience of negative energy did, does, and will continue to have profound horrific consequences on humanity. We can call that Satan, an energy adverse to our own best interest. Let's dig deeper.

I say "more than likely a mythical creature" with the following back up. First, the word "Satan" in the original Hebrew does simply mean "adversary" and is used many times throughout the Old Testament as such. The word does not appear in Genesis at all. So the deceptive "serpent," which may be a reference to the word for "leviathan," or sea serpent used in other parts of the Bible, is not regarded at all as Satan. In fact, the definite article "Satan" appears only twice in the entire Old Testament: first in the Book of Job, which is a work of literature, and second in the Book of Zechariah, both again describing an adversarial position.

It should be noted that both of those books have been dated to the time of Babylonian captivity and the second temple period, where Jewish culture was highly influenced by the Zoroastrianism religion of the Achaemenids.[7] Jewish conceptions of Satan as devil evolved from "Ahriman," the Zoroastrian god of evil and . . . ignorance, while additionally other constructs developed simultaneously, including heaven, hell, angels, demons, and end times beliefs.[8]

Additionally, Jewish pseudepigrapha flourished during the second temple period. These are are falsely attributed works: text whose claimed author is not the true author or a work whose real author attributed it to a figure of the past. These include the Book of Enoch, Book of Jubilees, Second Book of Enoch, and the Book of Wisdom, all non-canonical writings that influenced writers and more importantly translators of the current Bible but were not deemed credible enough to include in canon. So, any Evangelical belief that the Bible is the inerrant, fully God-inspired Word is false, according to their own doctrine.

Further, I am convinced that all references in the New Testament to Satan are either allegorical, used to describe an adversarial/accusatory narrative or mistranslated by "devil-forward" theologians on a mission. For example, 1 John 5:18–19 reads, "We know that anyone born of God does not continue to sin; the One who was born of God keeps them safe, and the evil one cannot

7. Kelly, *Satan*, 21.

8. Shapero, "Zoroastrianism," 4.

harm them. We know that we are children of God, and that the whole world is under the control of the evil one."[9]

Poneros is the Greek term translated as "evil one" but means "hardships, toils, annoyances, perils, etc." *Ketai* is Greek for "lies, laid, set, etc.," and is included in the Greek phrase. *Haptetai* is the Greek meaning "to touch or change in a way that alters them." The passage could then be translated as: "We know that anyone born of God does not continue to intentionally miss the target; Christ keeps them safe, so that no peril will ever change them permanently. We know that we are children of God, and that the whole world is filled with peril."

That is an absolutely true and beautiful statement from John. No need for fire and brimstone. John is saying that the world is filled with horror, but Christ protects those striving to hit the mark and that no permanent harm will come to them. It is clear that we could have a very different Bible today from start to finish that just might have led to a much more peaceful, loving world. But we chose hell, yet again. Free will holds the devil in the details.

Speaking of fire and brimstone, let's take a quick look at hell in the Bible. The following are the only references to hell in the New Testament, save for one reference in James, chapter three, speaking to the power of the tongue. All other references are from Jesus, but the word in question is *Gehenna*, which has been translated to mean hell.

Gehenna is an actual place, just south and west of Jerusalem. It is the Valley of Hinnom, the literal translation of Gehenna.[10] It has a torrid history as a place of child sacrifice to idolatrous gods. It has also been an ever-burning trash dump, hence the description of eternal hellfire. Regardless, Gehenna was well known to the hearers of Jesus' parables and was not a good place at all, unless you were taking out the trash. Also, local wild dogs gnashed their teeth fighting for scraps in Gehenna. Sound familiar? Let's look at these specific verses and replace the word "hell" with the words "trash" or "trash dump" meaning to make oneself useless or unfit to serve.

9. 1 John 5:18–19, NIV.

10. Bell, *Love Wins*, 67.

In Matt 5, Jesus says, "Anyone who says, 'You fool!' will be in danger of the trash dump (being useless to the cause)," and also, "It is better for you to lose one part of your body than for your whole body to be thrown into the trash (to be unfit to serve)." In Matt 10 and again in Luke 12 he says, "Be afraid of the One who can destroy both soul and body in the trash dump (making oneself useless)." In Matt 18 and Mark 9, Jesus says, "It is better for you to enter life with one eye than to have two eyes and be thrown into the trash (and be useless)."

Lastly, In Matt 23, he warns religious leaders that they win converts and make them "twice as much a child fit for the trash dump (as a useless tool)" as they already are, and then asks them, "How will you escape being condemned to the trash heap (as useless tools)?"

Jesus was a skilled communicator and had a sharp tongue that could cut straight to the heart and drop "sinners" to their knees. He could also go right for the jugular of the self-righteous pharisees. However, he spoke every word in the spirit of love and righteousness.

He used hyperbole and graphic imagery in his speech, which was not uncommon, as that is exactly how people in the East communicated truths and concepts, as we explored in the last chapter. What was uncommon about Jesus is that he spoke with authority. All these verses are clearly indicating that it is better to be imperfect but be a "really useful engine," to quote *Thomas the Tank Engine*, than to feign perfection and be a useless tool.

He could be quite a crack-up as well. Look at Matt 7:3 that reads, "You can see the speck in your friend's eye, but you don't notice the log in your own eye."[11] It is actually my favorite Scripture because you get a real sense of the historic man.

Another word, *tartarus*, is used once in 2 Peter, wherein Peter conjured up Greek mythology, describing the underworld. Lastly, the Greek *Hades*, which is interchangeable with the Hebrew *Sheol*, the resting place of the dead, is used in Rev 1, 6, and 20 and in Acts 2.

11. Matt 7:3, NIV.

God is a God of restoration, not eternal retribution. We see it in the letters of Paul, where in frustration he tells his friends to "hand over to Satan" followers who continue in sin without fail. What he is saying is, "Give him over to his own devices until he comes to his senses." We see this also in Matt 25, in the parable of the sheep and the goats, wherein the goats are sent to an "*aion of kolazo*," a time of pruning and correction.[12]

Let's go back to Eden where we first chose hell. Yes, the story is an allegory wrapped in truth, but it is quite profound. Creation is God's first revelation to humanity. We naturally intuit that God is both creator and integrated into our planet and universe. Creation is the result of God's love. Love feels good. Creation feels good. Human reproduction, in turn, feels good, because it is a form of physical creation. Weirdly, humanity can be described as "user generated" similarly to how we use social media. Think about it. Facebook is just a big empty version of the universe without our user-generated content that fills up billions upon billions of posts and pages. So, humanity was created to perpetuate creation.

In Eden humanity was One with God in a unitive connection, just as in the word I created, "Infiunity," describing exactly that. The knowledge of good and evil refers to humanity's use of free will to pull away from that oneness with God to act exclusive to it. So, with one bite of fruit from that tree, paradise was lost.

Let's dig into the truth behind the creation story and interpret it more literally. After tasting the fruit, Adam and Eve were cast out and condemned to forge a new life without God's help. Since then, humanity attempted to rebuild Eden from scratch. My how far we have come in the last several thousand years. But are we remotely close to Utopia?

If you stripped away every iota of civilization, culture, shelter, personal accoutrements, even down to eyeglasses and toilet paper (Can I get an amen, my fellow pandemicians?); no cars, no electricity, no fire; no nothing at all but your absolute naked existence on a wild planet Earth; what you are left with is your spirit and a temporary mortal housing unit of limited natural mobility.

12. Bell, *Love Wins*, 91.

Adam and Eve were one hundred percent dependent on God for everything. In turn, everything needed was supplied by God in Eden. If the veil of our civilization were ripped off today, we would discover that we remain billions of Adams and Eves, rebuilding Eden for our very survival. Life on this planet is truly paradise lost.

It could be argued that humanity created its own hell right then and there in Eden. The wage of sin was and is death. Death to the oneness with God. Death of the human body. Death of Eden. Mankind was forced to recreate its way back to security and a false security at best. Conceiving a new life on a wild planet using nothing but tools and weapons of stone and clothes made of animals, skinned as blood sacrifices to cover our "nakedness," was no easy task.

Humanity lost eternal life and a deep connection to the source of everything. That is a deep loss. But just look what we have built in its place! Oy. We are closer to nuclear annihilation than paradise.

Judaism is a perfect example of how impossible it was/is to work our way back to a restorative unity with God. Life under the law was dreadful and required much of the faithful. As 2 Cor 3:6 reads, "a new covenant, not of letter but of spirit; for the letter (of the law) kills, but the spirit gives life."[13]

The Jews failed time and again to live up to God's standards. So Jesus, the Jewish Messiah, was offered to the world to restore unity and died in solidarity with mankind to save it from itself as the risen Christ. So, in Adam, all die, therefore in Christ, the second Adam, all live, as Jesus cried on the cross, "It is accomplished." If not one word was ever written in any Bible, "It is accomplished." Jesus never wrote a single word. It does not matter, "It is accomplished." The kingdom is "now" in the risen Christ. The kingdom is forever. The kingdom is inside you and beyond time and space in eternity, in an ever-present . . . present.

Century upon century, theologians expanded a disparate network of concepts that developed into the singular current metanarrative of systematic theology, dispensationalism, and salvation

13. 2 Cor 3:6, NIV.

by stringing together obscure and difficult passages and subjective interpretative translation. It is self-evident that Satan and hell are integral to that concept. To that end, hell is too big to fail. If hell goes away, so goes Churchianity with it, positioned on fear of hell and the devil's pitchfork.

Strictly established on current evidence, I am championing an evolved faith to emerge, not at the expense of truth, but because of it. Understanding of truth, much like science, can evolve or is proved through modern research, analysis, and experimentation. As noted previously, debate and competing theologies are as much a part of the Judeo/Christian tradition as Christmas and Easter. This book humbly asks to be included in that debate. It is simply time for the love, mercy, and grace of Christ to take the theological reigns in the twenty-first century.

7

Seven Deadly Sins, but Who's Counting?

IT IS NO SECRET among friends that long before my official break with Churchianity, the late great planet Jerry Falwell baited my ire, which will be self-evident, if not already. In retrospect, I most definitely observed cracks in the foundation of my practiced faith with its morally superior theocratic agenda twenty years ago.

Also, I am painfully aware of the ad hominem slam I just laid on a deceased man, but I promise there is a method to my madness. It does not sound very gracious coming from the man I claim to be *en Christo*, does it? It could be construed as a compliment, as for a few decades Falwell was a larger-than-life prominent global figure, while millions of devotees orbited his presence. But it was not a compliment. You know it and I know it. I do give him props, but the props end with his successful run at shouting above the noise to be seen and heard nationally. Speaking of homonyms, you could say that Falwell is just a prop in this hit piece on selective sin among the brethren.

As a kid, I first encountered Falwell in the parodied caricature of him on an episode of the '70s TV series, *WKRP in Cincinnati*. The pompous, self-righteous glutinous mass presented on the tube created a conflict in my young malleable mind. Say what you will, but TV can influence heads of mush, and mine was a big bowl of oatmeal. I presumed the demeanor of the comedic portrayal must have been exaggerated as my understanding of Jesus, even at that tender age, did not align. Unfortunately, the media was correct in this case, as I investigated the Moral Majority and found nothing more but modern-day pharisaic bombast. Yet, its influence corrupted many denominations under the banner of Evangelicalism, including my own.

Let us go back to the future circa 1997. Falwell came out as a homophobe when he slammed celebrity Ellen DeGeneres for coming out as a homosexual. He decided in his infinite wisdom to condemn the "sinner, not the sin" by launching an *ad hominem* public assault calling her "Ellen DeGenerate." It was not very gracious of the man he claimed to be *en Christo*, was it? Listen, Ellen does not need me to defend her on a quarter-century plus old gay-shame. That is not where I'm going.

But Falwell's exegetical excretion, all part and parcel of his "suppository" preaching, was in fact very bad news for modern man. I equate Falwell's egregious attack on a civilian as a setback to Christianity on par with the crusades. True, not a soul was killed in combative jousting matches this time around, but the bad PR in the age of mass media was not inconsequential. It had a negative effect on an entire generation of current and prospective faithful, not to mention the organized rage machine that the LGBTQ community unleashed, and rightfully so. Falwell acted, and as such was nothing more than a schoolyard bully.

Ellen is a grown up and secure in her identity, of course, but Falwell lacked the spiritual foresight and personal integrity to deduce that she has an eternal soul just like his, yours, and mine. His unwarranted bigoted anti-Christian remarks cut me to the core. I was infuriated but had no national voice to scream from the rooftops or issue a sincere apology to Ellen on behalf of all thinking, feeling, allied disciples around the globe. I do now, sort of, so I am sorry, Ellen.

Churchianity's stance on homosexuality is fueled by the fear-based little "g" gospel blasted from pulpits around the US. However, the leading proselytizers appear to be more terrified of the gay community than the fires of hell. Why? Lust for power. The truth: the rank and file of Churchianity live in fear of the slightest fray in the delicate fabric of faith they have woven into the quilt of American culture. If the LGBTQs gain power, then theirs will unravel, and these people worship at the altar of power.

I am not going to deep dive on the scant lines of Scripture that relate to homosexual acts. That is not where I'm going, either. Suffice to say that all sex outside of a committed relationship would be considered sin in the Bible, that much is clear. The question is why is it sin? Further, the Bible under current management is not going to stop people, even the faithful, from having sex outside of marriage or from the random hook-up for that matter. Evangelicals have zero credibility, that much is also clear.

As humanity is baptized in the sophisticated postmodern open society afforded to much of the world, it is easy to fall into the belief that all consensual sex is quite alright and does no harm if practiced responsibly and safely. No one has considered that last sentence more than me since I turned, say, fifteen. I am no exception or saint in that respect, nor will any judgement be imposed on my part.

But the truth is all sex, even inside of marriage, has consequences. It is risky business, but a good one if you can get it. I remember a line the late comic genius Robin Williams delivered that went something like, "Men spend nine months trying to escape a vagina, then spend the rest of their lives trying to get right back in." Truth.

God created sex to enable humanity to in turn become creators in the propagation of future generations of humanity. We are user generated creations who continue the process into a forever of tomorrows. Sex in a committed relationship is also a living metaphor for the oneness created in communion with God.

We intuitively know the "perils" of sex. In a committed relationship, ill-timed pregnancies, conception, and contraception issues, and even miscommunication of desire all factor in but are worth the price of admission. All are part and parcel of the deal of commitment and bonding.

Sex outside of commitment creates a facsimile of the oneness experience, but is severed like a machete to the soul, leaving gaping emotional wounds when a split occurs, which causes a deeper heart-breaking level of betrayal in divorce. God's love for us is the reason for calling it "sin" or missing the mark. It is one target we should all strive to hit. God is not some sadistic killjoy. Divorce and sex outside of committed long-term relationships are called out as sin for our own benefit to escape that pain. I am convinced that the agony of separation in the severing of the oneness in a break-up is a crystal-clear immersive metaphor for what separation from God is like. That is a hell that most of us have experienced at least once, if not many times in this life. It is a primer for the hell we will create for ourselves in the continued rejection of God's unrelenting pursuit to love each one of us.

So, what does that say about all sin in God's eyes? Sin is sin and it is called sin for the benefit of avoidance of unnecessary pain and anguish. That is pretty awesome when you think about it! But why do practitioners of Churchianity focus so much on lust and neglect the other six deadly sins? Well for starters, wrath, pride, and greed are part and parcel of following and achieving the American dream. So, back off there, buddy boy.

Additionally, sloth, number six on our countdown, means more than just being lazy. It can also be ascribed to neglecting to do what is right in the face of injustice. We must stand up for what is good and true. Hint, there was always more at stake in American politics than the abortion cause, which let's face it, most anti-abortion voters merely cast a vote once every four years for the politician who talked the best game. That is a perfect description of sloth. However, Evangelicals lost all pro-life street cred when they donned "my body, my choice" t-shirts in protest of the "tyranny" of stay-at-home orders when asked to be their brother's keeper during the pandemic.

The judgmental, hate-fueled practice of going after the sinners and not the sin is a losing and shameful strategy, as the "opponent" rather than the "human person with an eternal soul" simply digs in their heels deeper. That is not the Gospel, but again is an example of sloth. Further, if the church did its job, as the light and love of Christ on Earth, the abortion rate could be exponentially decreased through a fusion of compassion and social services providing education, birth control, and empathy without a single vote being cast or court case overturned. Personally, I have evolved to become a pro-choice anti-abortionist, believing that abortion should be legal, safe, restrictive, and rare. As science evolves, which already includes Plan B, the morning after pill, new technologies and pharmaceuticals will emerge as widely accepted ethical alternatives that will prevent not only unwanted pregnancy, but the mental health issues that plague those who have considered or had abortions. This stance frees me from the bondage of single-issue exclusivity to the GOP voting bloc.

That leaves us with gluttony. Oh, where to begin? It is plausible to assume that the number one sin in America is gluttony. Obesity, alcoholism, and drug addiction are the number one direct or indirect causes of premature death in the US. We self-soothe and self-medicate in the overindulgence of food, drink, and drug daily, just to cope with the other six deadly sins that compete with our attention and addiction in pursuit of life, liberty, and happiness.

That brings us back to our prop, Mr. Falwell. In his understanding of God's rules, A+B=C. So in relation to homosexuality, dying in sin while practicing with no regard for the consequence of sin leads to hell. By his own standards, it stands to reason that he, as a morbidly obese man, died in sin of heart issues related to obesity, while practicing sin with no regard for the consequence thereof, in this case, gluttony. So in fact Jerry Falwell is in hell with all the homos.

To be clear, I am being deceptively cheeky here, but you get the point, right? I do not believe Jerry Falwell is in hell, nor do I believe "all the homos" are there, either. In an interesting side bar, an anecdote attributed to Julian of Norwich, a Christian mystic of the fourteenth century was once asked publicly if she believed in hell. The official reply ascribed to her was "yes," and then whispered secretly to friends, "but I don't believe anyone is there." Such is life as a servant of the Catholic Church, but I like that sentiment.

If sin is sin, then all sin is equal in the eyes of God. We cannot hand-pick sins to adjudicate or deem one as "more" evil over the other regardless of culture, society, or individual inclinations or proclivities, regardless of genetics or predisposition. Genetics and environment both play significant roles in our individual, tribal, and collective development, thus it stands that we are just one big beautiful hot mess.

No one is immune from moral failure. I think all rational people are willing to admit that. The good news is the Gospel of Christ is all inclusive. There are no missed targets that grace has not already adjudicated and declared forgiven. After several millennia of an ever-evolving human race, which is a reality God set in motion generations ago, there are myriad flaws and facets of life beyond individual control, without medical, psychological, or spiritual intervention. So, "Let he who is without sin, cast the first stone."[1]

Jesus summed up and fulfilled the Law and the Prophets (the entire Old Testament) as the risen Christ, with the paraphrase, "Love God and love people." In Mark 12:30–31, he gave us a revolutionary commandment that transcended time and religion when he stated, "Love your neighbor as yourself." In many circumstances, we forget to love ourselves or cannot forgive ourselves, so we are rendered incapable of loving others. If we hate ourselves, we cannot love our neighbors. Taking Falwell as an example, it is quite possible the man was riddled with self-loathing, ate his emotions, and lashed out at "sinners" in a subconscious effort to appeal to an under-inflated ego, as unbelievable as that sounds, which presented as pompous asininity.

Loving oneself is not a prescription for selfishness, but it is one for positive self-care and inner ego work required of each of us to be able to love our neighbor. We are loved by God, each one

1. John 8:7, NIV.

of us. So then, please choose to "love God, love people, and love yourself." Those seven words give us all the gumption to overcome the seven deadly sins.

8

The Inner Revolution of Christ

JESUS WAS A REVOLUTIONARY teacher and master communicator, but you would think all he ever did was, you know, save the world as the living Christ. His teachings were authoritative, profound, at times subversive, and many times wrapped inside a parable, but today are overshadowed by Churchianity's fear-based gospel and hyper-focused on the atonement narrative. "Whoever has ears, let them hear," as so stated in Matt 11:15.[1] Worse still, Christ's precepts have either been conscripted into the agenda of religious nationalism, aka Churchianity, if in alignment with the Pauline letters that is, or dismissed out of hand for being nuanced or difficult.

The Jewish religious leaders of the first century condemned Jesus to death in part because they misread the times and misinterpreted their own Scripture to suit an agenda, in seeking a political messiah. Today, the powers behind religious nationalism would enforce a US theocracy if given the opportunity, in misreading the times and misinterpreting Scripture, which by the way does not even fit their own apocalyptic metanarrative. Next year, Jeru—err, wait, Washington! What, I can't make with the jokes?

---

1. Matt 11:15, NIV.

This might be as good of a time as any to clearly state that I love the Jewish people and deeply empathize with the plight and suffering they have endured for centuries as God's Chosen. It was not easy being God's Chosen, but the Jewish people held a central place in the unitive history of God and humanity, most notably in suffering, and as an example to the rest of the world.

Being God's Chosen made them much more vulnerable to misery because a suffering humanity sees beyond the natural into the eternal. In other words, we learn better and take to heart spiritual truths in times of anguish rather than in times of great joy. In fact, there could be no joy without suffering (or wine, in paraphrasing a Jewish proverb). This "liminal space" is a time of grace that feels like anything but grace. Pain, suffering, and loss characterize this place of "unlearning" and deep sorrow, where a fresh perspective propels us to new frontiers.

The incarnation of Jesus, as he stated, did not abolish, but fulfilled the Law and the Prophets (The Old Testament) as the risen Christ. That means something, doesn't it? Fundamentalists misrepresent that phrase to co-opt the letter of the law to weaponize the word. But clearly, Jesus is teaching us in the Sermon on the Mount (Matt 5) that the spiritual message of love, grace, and mercy behind the law is how we are to conduct our lives, as Jesus fulfilled the law in his suffering, death, and resurrection.

We can certainly source the Old Testament as a means of understanding how God interacted with the nation of Israel. We can also use it as a reassurance of God's promises and prophecy fulfilled, understand Israel's history, and immerse ourselves in its literature and teachings. Most of all, when studied in the context of the Bible as a whole, the OT helps us to see how God's plan was fulfilled in the death and resurrection of Christ and in the failing of Israel, culminating in the complete destruction of the nation in 70 AD. Israel was a failed first-century theocracy by God's own hand (with the assistance of the Roman military). The significance of that complete and brutal destruction that caused the Diaspora of the entire Hebrew nation is staggering. Just as Jesus cried out on the cross, "It is accomplished," it was all accomplished in the same generation that did not pass away, as he foretold in Matt 24.

What we cannot do is co-opt the Old Testament to shame, scandalize, or humiliate. We cannot promote or lobby an agenda of bigotry or offer it up as a scapegoat for violence. We most assuredly cannot adopt obscure passages to create an end times eschatology or invent a fear-forward gospel. We are in Christ under a new covenant with God.

Life under Roman rule was miserable, merciless, and brief. The Romans after all created and perfected the science of cruel torture and crucifixion. Even debt in those days of subsistence farming and basic skilled trades could easily chain up a family into slavery or worse. Jesus the revolutionary spoke into existence a message of radical inner freedom to those trapped under oppressive bondage.

He taught in parables, but with expressed love and kindness. His mission to the marginalized in Galilee was empathetic, compassionate, and pastoral. Upon arrival in Jerusalem, Jesus faced the oppressors of the marginalized. His message was sharp and cut like a sword of righteousness.

In Mark 11:17, Jesus entered the temple and violently overturned the merchant tables and the status quo, which enraged the pharisees who depended on that income as it was the Amazon of ancient Israel. "Money changers" converted foreign money into local currency so pilgrims could purchase animal sacrifices for temple worship. It sounds egregiously barbaric to modern minds, but unless you are vegan you might cozy up to the concept a bit more. The sacrifices were usually cooked and eaten by the offerer and were mainly used to commune or get closer to God. Atonement or scapegoating full animal sacrifice was limited, but it did occur.

Jesus was angered over the commercial activity, which transpired mainly in the Gentile courtyard, an open forum to discuss and debate religion. "My house will be called a house of prayer for all nations. But you have made it a den of robbers,"[2] Jesus exclaimed in Mark 11:17, as he "ethically cleansed" the temple, which

2. Mark 11:17, NIV.

was the catalyst that condemned him to death in less than a week (depending on which of the four Gospels you are reading). Always follow the money and threat to power.

In contrast, Jesus praised the faith of a Roman centurion, who believed the LORD could heal his servant, with only a word, miles from his home. He said in Matt 8:10, "Truly I tell you; I have not found anyone in Israel with such great faith."[3] So even then in his earthly life, before the resurrection and apostolic debate years later, Jesus clearly accepted the faith of Gentiles, even the most despised Romans.

The Jews hoped and prayed for a political and military messiah to free them from the tyranny of Rome, but Jesus showed them that the real oppression came from within. He presented an inner freedom to revolutionize their lives in love and unity with God. Jesus said in Luke 17:21, "For indeed, the kingdom of God is within you."[4] Today, we can tap into that inner freedom through Christ, as they did two thousand years ago, which exists simultaneously in eternity and in the ever present now.

All you must do is . . . die.

No, not physical death, but it might be good to note that although, yes, physical death is inevitable, we never lose spiritual/soul consciousness in the transition from life to life. The key to that seamless, even joyful transition is to die today and every day to the ego, to the self.

When you can "observe your true self behind your ego/persona," you are on your way there. You can get "there" through quiet inner prayer and contemplation, which is a form of meditation. To be still and know in the quiet presence of God is a natural state of human "being." But mankind always needs to slap a moniker to every "thing" so if you like, call it meditation, call it contemplation, or call it an Uber, it does not matter.

Jesus absolutely taught prayer beyond words: praying in secret (Matt 6:5–6), not babbling on (Matt 6:7), because your Father knows what you need before you ask (Matt 6:8). These all speak to

3. Matt 8:10, NIV.
4. Luke 17:21, NIV.

a deep contemplation, an inner place in space/time where eternity is present and oneness (infiunity) with God occurs in prayer without words. In the silence, we find fullness in the emptiness.

When we empty ourselves in solidarity with Jesus who emptied himself to save us, in becoming united to God by grace, through the Spirit, or as Jesus called it, "the Comforter," we are then filled with grace, resulting in oneness with God. It is in detaching from attachments to people, things of this world, thoughts, and ego (who you perceive as yourself) that drives this transcendence. No, it is not a call for stoicism or to hermitage in cloister at all, as you can only genuinely enjoy your life on Earth when untethered in absolute freedom under grace.

"Attachment to spiritual things is just as much an attachment as inordinate love of anything else," said the late Father Thomas Merton, a cloistered Trappist Monk in his 1961 book, *New Seeds of Contemplation*.[5] Yes, even religion, faith, and spirituality can be an idol, inasmuch as who you parade around as yourself (your ego) can too. The ability to see yourself behind the eyes of your ego is fundamental.

To illustrate, let's discuss a profound dream I recently experienced. I was walking to my car, which was an expensive silver Audi R8, parked in a country club parking lot. I noticed that a caretaker had placed a white plastic bottle of bleach on the trunk lid. Infuriated at the injustice of it all, I became enraged, grabbed the open bottle, and promptly splashed its contents, staining my shirt and cardigan. Maybe I was Mr. Rogers in this dream, as I would never wear a cardigan, but not to digress.

It turns out that the bottle did not, in fact, contain bleach, but gasoline. Therefore, I was not marked by fresh scented purity, but baptized in stinky gasoline, so that people might consider me as beneath my station, uncool, or perhaps, duh-duh-duh . . . as a charlatan. I hightailed it to the "manager's" office to complain, but there were hundreds of people all trying to get on the same elevator up to "his" office, while shouting out their complaints. So,

---

5. Merton, *New Seeds*, 205–6.

I attempted to shout over them with my complaint and to justify my soiled appearance.

In the next scene I found myself and others sitting in a cozy, well-appointed waiting room. I am silent but aggravated by yet another wait to offer my grievance, clearly a metaphor with my impatience with God, err, the manager. I observed the Dalai Lama sitting across from me. He was silent but smiling. I did not speak a word but offered a nod of approval of recognition. Kind of a "s'up?" to the great man of Buddhism.

He said, "You are very angry." I replied, "It hides my sadness." He asked, "Why are you sad?" I replied, "Because everything should be perfect, but it isn't." He said nothing else, but gazed at me in silence, with a warm glowing smile. I reciprocated and peace fell over me.

In our silence, we observed that in the presence of the Presence Beyond the Universe, everything is perfect in that moment, both in time and beyond time. When we are in the presence of God, we are in eternity as well as in space/time. This is an example of what Jesus meant when he said, "The kingdom of God is within you," as noted above. It is also kind of cool that the Dalai Lama was waiting to meet with the manager, too.

I woke up (figuratively and literally) and pondered a proverb of sorts that came to me some time before, while in a state of meditation. That sounds super spiritual; however, I can assure you, it was not. But here goes: "Wisdom means living the essence of truth. Knowledge of truth is just a false positive."

In other words, our lives in this world, living in the shallows, are filled with imperfection, delusion, and at times abject horror. We can accumulate knowledge and wealth, but if we don't apply that knowledge or properly deal with wealth (Matt 19:4) it amounts to nothingness.

We can escape this world anytime, while still living in it, by leaning into and acknowledging the presence, or the kingdom, or Christ in the moment. In that moment, all is perfection as oneness. This is what it means to live in the world, but not be of the world. In so doing, we are free and living wisdom. So then, the

Scripture, 1 John 2:15, has little to do with being separate to live a self-righteous morality. Our peace that passes all understanding lives in the Presence, in that moment.

But that peace must prevail throughout our work-a-day lives, too. And good luck to you. It ain't easy, yet it is—if mindfulness is activated by your minute-by-minute thinking. Be mindful to flow through the day or the issue or the pain or the anxiety. True, it sometimes requires breaking down walls to flow through them. There are hard days indeed and "hard day's nights," wrote the late John of Liverpool.

Try this on for an exercise in faith to empty yourself and get to that place of oneness with God. Pray/meditate on Christ in silence and in gratitude for existence, or Ps 46:10, "Be still and know that I AM God."[6] You can also meditate on the mantra of the Eastern Orthodox Church which I humbly simplified even further, "Jesus, Son of the Living God, have mercy on me." I removed the words, "a sinner" because it is intuitively implied. Repeat the words aloud, then quieter, and finally internalize the words. Focus and be immersed in the oneness.

Recall that your very breath praises God or YHWH as you inhale "YH" and exhale "WH." Contemplate and acknowledge God's eternal and ever-present communion with you in an infinuity of love wrapped in and around you, your life, in everything and everyone (so you can see Christ in all), in the universe and beyond, as oneness. Let go of the false narrative that is your ego/persona/thoughts to spend time out of time in the ever present as God created you to be. When you know that you know that God is in you as you are in God, as God is in everyone and everything in the universe and beyond, then you are "there."

Live in that space as often as you can, until it becomes your natural state in times of joy, stress, illness, and God help us, even traffic.

Are we there yet?

---

6. Ps 41:10, NIV.

9

How Should We Live Then?

It could be argued that everything we need to know about living in Christ can be learned in the 1965 cartoon classic, *A Charlie Brown Christmas*. In fact, we could just stop right here, watch it on Apple+, let the wisdom sink in, and call it a day.

I have watched religiously every year since I could crawl. The annual holiday special, especially my beloved early Hostess Twinkie–sponsored CBS showings in the '70s, were and always will be central to my Christmas tradition (which, truth be told, usually ramps up around *Great Pumpkin* time). Up until recently, however, I missed something stunningly profound (for a 1960s animated special) interwoven into the cartoon.

Linus Van Pelt, brother to Lucy and BFF to good ol' Charlie Brown, is widely known to cling to his security blanket day and night. But while delivering his monologue on the meaning of Christmas, quoting Luke 2:8–14, he speaks the words, "Fear not!" and drops the blanket to the stage floor. It is subtle, but it is there, and it is awesome. It is a clear message to those of us who are not watching our flocks by night that we also must "fear not" as we walk through life to take the risk to love our neighbors as ourselves, face challenging times, and live our lives abundantly.

True, Linus clings to that blanket again after delivering the message, which is indicative of the struggle to remain strong, but at the end of the day, his blanket is offered as the skirt to the tragically beautiful tree Charlie Brown chose to represent Christmas. We are all tragically beautiful, damaged, and broken in one way or another, but we are grounded in the security blanket of God. A few of us know that truth and are secure in the peace that passes all understanding. Others do not, but desperately need to know and trust that it is so.

To that end, I refer to the last chapter's proverb, "Wisdom is living the essence of truth. Knowledge of truth is just a false positive." In other words, applied knowledge, if that knowledge is true and good, is considered wisdom and we should immerse ourselves inside that truth and live it daily.

Pilate asked Jesus, "*Quid est veritas?*" or "What is Truth?" Let us look at the exchange in John 18:36–38. "You are a king, then!" said Pilate. Jesus answered, "You say that I am a king. In fact, the reason I was born and came into the world is to testify to the truth. Everyone on the side of truth listens to me." "What is truth?" retorted Pilate. But Pilate didn't wait for his answer. Jesus was flogged and crucified.[1]

Love is truth inasmuch as God is love and it is a powerful force when unleashed on the world. Love enabled Jesus to endure thirty-nine lashes and compelled him to remain nailed to a tree to save the world as the risen Christ. Love is the power that moves the sun and other stars, according to Dante. Love was and is the force behind the propagation of the human race for millennia and will be for millennia to come. Love serves those who cannot or will not love back.

Contrary to the circumstantial evidence we face in the daily news, love that drives empathy and compassion is literally built into our DNA as humans. We were born to be our "brother's keeper." In fact, recent studies (see HeartMath.Org) proved that when we do good things for others our hearts radiate an electromagnetic field of love. Subsequently, when we see others suffering,

1. John 18:36–38, NIV.

we suffer ourselves. Love is good for the heart as it beats out a real physiological message when acting out in love and endorphins are released in the brain when we do good.

We are all one interconnected people. This fact should propel us to move in concert with each other to change the world. Unfortunately, human civilization is focused on greed, power, and self-interest. These are traits diametrically opposed to who we really are at the core.

Could we transform a world riddled with hatred into a utopia of love and compassion, where the global common good is the centerpiece of civilization? Yes, in the fullness of love, as we have studied thus far, oh yes, we can. It may take three hundred years, but it can be accomplished.

In choosing the path of love, we can help those deeply damaged individuals seeking to destroy or oppress, to see the truth to become fully healed humans. When Jesus said in Matt 5:39, "Turn the other cheek," he meant this exact action. Is it easy? No. Can it be done on a governmental level? Not currently. It is accomplished one-on-one, individually and locally, built out to national or global scale. Small everyday acts of kindness offered to those we have no vested interest in other than to better their world or life situation (Matt 5:47), in large or small ways, multiplied over and over can scale exponential positive change throughout the world.

Case in point is the Evangelical epic moral failure to flip Rowe v. Wade through self-righteous bullying, lobbying, and political power grabs. The strategy begot nothing but a blot on Christianity and left a bad taste in the mouths of opponents who simply dug in their heels. A victory, yes, but at what cost?

If you believe you have the moral high ground on an issue and want to effect change, it can only be accomplished with love as the driver or it will fail spiritually. If you cannot see and feel the pain in another's eyes, you will lose, not only the contest, but your moral high ground as well, whether individually or in a national movement. And there will always be consequences. Yes, blessed are the peacemakers, but they don't get much airplay anymore.

It breaks down to this:

Love like you want to be loved. Forgive like you want to be forgiven. Offer grace and mercy to those who may not be capable of or willing to give it back to you. Be generous with all you have, even if you think you have nothing to offer, you can offer kindness. Take risks and live now, not in the past or tomorrow. In that now, as discussed in the previous chapter, you can connect with God and in that oneness can accomplish anything. While in that space, "Ask and it will be given to you; seek and you will find; knock and the door will be opened to you."[2]

Many, many people are not evolved spiritually, emotionally, or psychologically. The "lost" are really just folks incapable of seeing the true self behind the ego/personality, but are absorbed into the world outwardly and inwardly, living life in the shallows. Jesus called the pharisees "blind guides." Bingo. They are people in the world and of the world. They can be religious or atheist.

In many cases they also become our best teachers. In fact, that pain in the flying buttress you try to avoid like the unmasked sneeze machine in the dairy aisle (see global pandemic 2020, 2021, 2022, and counting) is exactly the person you need to deal with and now. If you delay, that person or that archetype will be a thorn in your side until you learn the lesson you need to learn.

In Mark 10, Jesus reached out in love to a rich man, who had "kept all the commandments all his life" and asked if he could be saved. Jesus, knowing the man was immersed in his wealth and living in the shallows, told him to go and sell everything for the poor and "follow me." The man walked away saddened, then Jesus said, "It is easier for a camel to go through the eye of a needle than for someone who is rich to enter the kingdom of God."

Jesus confirmed that the rich man was "lost" as is described above. It means that the man cannot see (or does not want to see or is oblivious to see) his true self beyond his ego/persona or find that oneness with God in the (inner) kingdom Jesus taught, due to his immersive love of things. It does not mean that man was condemned to eternal hellfire. Note that the man "kept" all the commandments, therefore was "righteous" in the eyes of the law,

2. Matt 7:7, NIV.

but his heart was not right. Jesus is all about heart. That one teaching alone hoists Churchianity on its own petard.

Let's talk about forgiveness, something I'm in need of on a daily basis. When you forgive someone's wrongdoing, it frees you, not the wrongdoer. However, empathy will be reciprocal on some level, but may not be readily apparent in the moment. It does not matter. You are freed indeed, and that person is on their own journey. Thus, your action will impact that journey, whether immediate or on a death bed or consciously or subconsciously. Every interaction causes a reaction and bears a resulting consequence, culminating in myriad outcomes for individuals and all humanity in a free will–centric world.

Forgiveness frees you from past built up negativity that constricts the flow of love and "positivity." Flow is good. When you harbor negative feelings, thoughts, and actions, which are all forms of energy, they create emotional and spiritual and potentially physical blockages. It is better to let all flow through, good and bad. In other words, you do not have to process each emotion or thought one by one by digging into your subconscious, like a mindfulness twelve-step program. Simply forgive in the flow of life as anything pops up, then your heart will be free. It helps to live mindfully behind thoughts and emotions, as the observer behind your own eyes and thoughts, as detailed in the last chapter.

Jesus says in Matt 6:34, "Do not worry about tomorrow, for tomorrow will worry about itself. Each day has enough trouble of its own."[3] The meaning: do not sweat the small stuff or the big stuff. Stuff includes all the negative thoughts you maintain and store that lead to worry about the future, the past, and the "what ifs." Engaging with all that shuts you down, but if you let it flow through as thoughts, actions, and situations come into your mind and environment, freedom and joy are yours.

Spiritual evolution removes blockages causing fear. To be certain, life presents fear-causing situations, but when you see those trials as an opportunity for growth you can flow through them. When

3. Matt 6:34, NIV.

fear is held close, you remain closed and insulate deeper, causing fear to replicate like a virus. So, surrender yourself and let go.

Practice emptying, as the bigger the conflict holding you down, once released, will make room for you to fill up more! Conversely, negativity attracts more negativity. True transformation begins when you see problems as agents for growth. Romans 12:2 reads, "Do not conform yourselves to the standards of this world, but let God transform you inwardly by a complete change of your mind."[4]

In Matt 7:3–5, Jesus says, "Why do you look at the speck of sawdust in your brother's eye and pay no attention to the plank in your own eye?"[5] Whether in battle with a Plankeye v. Speckeye or a Plankeye v. Plankeye, real emotional damage is inflicted on real human emotion, so be mindful of indignation, petty or otherwise, to maintain an environment of grace and empathy.

Attitude is key when confronted with conflict of all kinds. It is not easy to avoid ruminating on conflict, nor can most issues be ignored. But, when you taste the exquisite peace of letting go and letting it flow through, you will be transformed. Be conscious of being conscious and soon the heart will subdue the mind and you will live in a state of love and liberation. Forgive, relax, and release. Freedom is on the other side of the exchange.

When you unhinge from all darkness, negative impulses, and attachments to the things of this world, you will be filled with light that overcomes all darkness and experience peace that passes all understanding. It is a commitment, but one most worth your effort. If you do stumble or miss the mark, say, "I am at peace and live in Christ," then let it go. In this state, while you remain inside time and space, eternity is simultaneously present in your heart. The kingdom within you is the kingdom to come on Earth as it is in heaven.

Jesus in Matt 18:3, said, "Truly I tell you, unless you change and become like little children, you will never enter the kingdom of heaven."[6] As children there is little concern for the future or past,

4. Rom 12:2, GNT.

5. Matt 7:3–5, NIV.

6. Matt 18:3, NIV.

only the present, which is a way of living in eternity beyond time and space, something humanity cannot truly grasp on the surface. As you change and become like a child to limit contemplation of what "is" in the now, all ghosts of regrets past and worries future evaporate, the kingdom of God is within you, and you and God are One. "That all of them may be one, Father, just as you are in me, and I am in you. May they also be in us so that the world may believe that you have sent me,"[7] Jesus prayed for all in John 17:21. In that fervent prayer, his expectation was unitive consciousness as One in God.

Lastly, we've clearly expressed throughout this book that "love is the answer." We've summed up the entire Bible as: "Love God, love people, and love yourself." But one could argue, and I suppose I will again, that contrary to the 24/7 news cycle of abject daily horror, a significant amount of love exists in this world already, so why hasn't love saved the day if love truly is the answer?

Because we truly don't know what to do with all that love. So, to parody an old Burt Bacharach song, "What the world needs now, is wisdom, sweet wisdom." Let's look at a teaching of Jesus commonly known as the "Parable of the Wheat and Tares."

> Jesus told them another parable: "The kingdom of heaven is like a man who sowed good seed in his field. But while everyone was sleeping, his enemy came and sowed weeds among the wheat, and went away. When the wheat sprouted and formed heads, then the weeds also appeared. The owner's servants came to him and said, 'Sir, didn't you sow good seed in your field? Where then did the weeds come from?' 'An enemy did this,' he replied. The servants asked him, 'Do you want us to go and pull them up?' 'No,' he answered, 'because while you are pulling the weeds, you may uproot the wheat with them. Let both grow together until the harvest. At that time I will tell the harvesters: First collect the weeds and tie them in bundles to be burned; then gather the wheat and bring it into my barn.'"[8]

7. John 17:21, NIV.
8. Matt 13:24–30, NIV.

Now let's read Jesus' own interpretation to his disciples, which clearly contains more mystery:

> Then he left the crowd and went into the house. His disciples came to him and said, "Explain to us the parable of the weeds in the field." He answered, "The one who sowed the good seed is the Son of Man. The field is the world, and the good seed stands for the people of the kingdom. The weeds are the people of the evil one, and the enemy who sows them is the devil. The harvest is the end of the age, and the harvesters are angels. As the weeds are pulled up and burned in the fire, so it will be at the end of the age. The Son of Man will send out his angels, and they will weed out of his kingdom everything that causes sin and all who do evil. They will throw them into the blazing furnace, where there will be weeping and gnashing of teeth. Then the righteous will shine like the sun in the kingdom of their Father. Whoever has ears, let them hear."[9]

Fourth century church father Gregory of Nyssa related how his sister, St. Macrina, interpreted this parable of hidden meaning, as Jesus concluded his private interpretation to his disciples with, "He who has ears to hear, let him hear." She concluded in my paraphrase that all humanity has the ability to love and war with each other and within our own selves. When we choose to be adversarial to our own being that war of unwise hatred and unwise wrongdoing grows within each of us intertwined with the love and goodwill we evoke. Therefore, we cannot weed out the chaff or tares of our own volition without destroying ourselves in so doing, as both are interlaced and strangling the roots. At the end of our lives, we will see ourselves as we truly are in judgment both by God and ourselves, leading to a gnashing of our own teeth in regret in a furnace of refining fire. But in the end, when God declares the "end of time" we will all achieve loving oneness with God in the life beyond.[10]

9. Matt 13:36–43, NIV.

10. Uebersax, "St. Macrina's Exegesis," para. 1–7.

Let's dissect what it means "to love" here on Earth. The word conjures a multitude of emotion and action. In love there is unspeakable joy, peace, contentment, meaningfulness, and mindfulness. But there is also deep fear, mourning, and grief of what may come in the loss of such love. There is sweet agony and ecstasy in the Greek terms for love including *eros*, but also in *agape* and *philia*. For example, every time I kiss my dog Liesel between the ears, I am filled with both joy and grief in understanding that her life is even shorter than my own. Love is bittersweet.

So even when we choose to act in love, there is so much packed into the word that acting with wisdom is at times unrealistic. We can act impulsively or jealously or empathetically, yet given the individual circumstances wisdom may or may not be present in those actions. Yet, we strive to be wise, to do good, and to be loving persons. Thus, not knowing what to do with all that love in the world is a fundamental problem and why there is so little wisdom.

So how shall we overcome these problems that are a threat to the very survival of humanity? Stop making our individuality more important than the whole of humanity. See the world behind your own eyes and ears, so you can see and hear with eyes that see and ears that hear. Pretend you have the eyes of God. Imagine you can observe the planet from outer space. What do you envision? You see thousands of babies born every second and thousands of people dying every second simultaneously, while in parallel the brevity of human life in its work-a-day toil of love and war appears frivolous on a good day. Yet, we all live in this mess. And we matter to God and to each other.

If we stopped seeking individual selfish meaning in our lives and instead focused on seeking meaning in offering goodwill in the community of humanity, we would become equally less important and more important individually in the collective consciousness of everyone when we work together for the common good. No, I am not a communist. I am a realist with an idealist complex simply trying to do my part to make the world a better place. What I am describing is anathema to the West, but in the East, this is the definition of meaningfulness.

Does anything you have just read sound like Churchianity? Evangelicalism? Fundamentalism? No, of course not, yet these are the direct teachings of Jesus. In fact, Jesus unfiltered by Churchianity resembles the Eastern wisdom teachings of Buddhism and Taoism and modern psychological therapy. That is remarkable and shows that science and Eastern tradition can complement faith in the twenty-first century because of his teachings, not because of a twisted bend to the will of biblical literalism to create a theocracy.

I provocatively named this chapter "How Should We Live Then?" in response to the identically titled works of Francis A. Shaeffer, who highly influenced power trippers like Jerry Falwell, founder of the Moral Majority as noted in chapter 1. Falwell and his contemporaries systematically devolved the faith into the politically partisan morality club of Churchianity. In John 10:30 Jesus claimed, "I and the Father are One," which sealed his fate as a blasphemer in direct conflict with the pharisees. Today, Churchianity proudly waves the same banner as postmodern pharisees in practice, doctrine, and political motivation (see the US Capitol insurrection of 2021). It is clear, these fundamentalists securely fit Jesus' description of pharisees as "white-washed tombs."

To that end, Churchianity must be repealed and replaced by love as the face of Christ to the world. The old song does not resound with, "They will know we are Christians by our bigotry." I contend that the world currently and rightly identifies many brands of Christianity as hate-filled right wingers. That is an egregious failure of the so-called church.

The thoughts and teachings I have expressed in these writings are not heretical. They are not unheard of or new. Many resemble the teachings of the Eastern Orthodox Church with over two 220 million worldwide members. Yet, if we are going to evolve the faith of the West past the brick hurricane that is Churchianity, we must remain steadfast in the security blanket of Christ, while daring to take the risk to be our brother's keeper, even if that brother is queer, on welfare, has dark skin, speaks Arabic, is a terrorist, or God forbid, a Democrat.

10

What If Rich Mullins Didn't Die?

"Jesus said, 'Whatever you do to the least of these my brothers you've done it to me.' And this is what I have come to think. That if I want to identify fully with Jesus Christ, who I claim to be my Savior and Lord, the best way that I can do that is to identify with the poor. This I know will go against the teachings of all the popular Evangelical preachers. But they are just wrong. They are not bad, they're just wrong. Christianity is not about building an absolutely secure little niche in the world where you can live with your perfect little wife and your perfect little children in a beautiful little house where you have no gays or minority groups anywhere near you. Christianity is about learning to love like Jesus loved and Jesus loved the poor and Jesus loved the broken-hearted."[1]

THAT WAS A QUOTE from Rich Mullins speaking at a concert of enraptured fans in Lufkin, Texas, on July 19, 1997, exactly sixty days before his excruciatingly untimely death. Amy Grant called Rich, "the uneasy conscience of Christian music."[2] I will expand

1. Mullins, "Rich Mullins Quote," para. 1.
2. GMA Dove Awards, "1998 Rich Mullins Tribute."

on that to proffer that Rich Mullins was the "uneasy conscience of Evangelicalism."

Rich was influenced by the late Brennan Manning, who penned the classic, equally loved and derided book, *The Ragamuffin Gospel*. Both Mullins and Manning were heavily influenced by St. Francis of Assisi, who is hardly the patron saint of Churchianity.

St. Francis taught a simple gospel of love, mercy, and grace epitomized in his identification with the poor. He was born into wealth but renounced it while he endured hardship and suffering in solidarity with the indigent. He is also the patron saint of ecology, something Churchianity has woefully abandoned. Francis founded the Franciscan Order and caused revival across Europe in the face of a corrupt church that lost its way.

I find it fascinating and ironic that two of the most beloved worship anthems of the last twenty years were composed by a Franciscan devotee in Mullins. "Awesome God" and "Sometimes by Step" are flawless works that evoke an immediate emotional response in anyone who empties their heart enough to identify that melancholic longing to connect with God.

The irony is that Mullins' beliefs and philosophy of life were the polar opposite of the overarching position of Evangelicalism in Western culture. Yet, at the heart of Sunday morning worship, congregants somehow briefly recognize their own Christ-starved parched lips and distended bellies, the result of barely surviving in a mercy desert. It saddens me as those "lost souls" immediately tamp down the pain of that desolate reality, to choose to live in outer darkness, void of the lush paradise of the kingdom of God within, through the vain pursuit of prosperity, a conservative nationalist American dream, and all of the accouterments that false narrative entails.

What if Rich Mullins didn't die? What influence would he have had on a post 9/11 church that was sucked deeply into the vortex of hyperactive nationalist fervor in a relentless pursuit to annihilate an enemy in need of Christ? What impact would Rich have had on President George W. Bush if he were spiritual advisor to the president (whom I've come to respect much more as a painter and post-presidential statesman)? How much leverage and credibility would the church have today on the influence of a national conscience relating to the pandemic, income inequality, race relations, culture, and hate-fueled political partisanship?

I am putting a lot on a dead rock star. But you get the point. It is not so much about what if Rich didn't die, but how far the church has devolved without him as an uneasy conscience to correct its path. To be truthful, not many were listening when he had a physical voice to shout in the wilderness or "Quote Deuteronomy to the devil." But his creations will live on forever.

The underlying issue is that there are no loud voices of conscience that can be heard over the din of prosperity-touting, bigoted, racist, homophobic, self-righteous, Trump adoring, white-washed tombs that are the face of Churchianity today. My goal is to rouse the rabble and raise up those voices to speak a message of truth, grace, mercy, and hope to the world in order to reimagine the face of Christianity as it was intended to be two thousand years ago. To that end, I'm making a clarion call for a total recall of this leading brand of Evangelicalism.

What do we build in its place?

We construct a new world with the face and hands of Jesus and a heart with the mind of Christ. It's simple, as it starts with you and me: "Love God, love people, and love yourself." These writings set the course for a rethink of everything as a primer for a meaningful, immersive, influential, and relevant postmodern civilization, beyond church.

No, I am not suddenly advocating for a global theocracy or caliphate. The Judaic laws were set forth as an example for all mankind. If Jesus fulfilled the law, then Christ is the salvation for the whole world. We just need the whole world to trust that it is "accomplished."

11

An Evolved Faith

IMMEDIATELY ON THE HEELS of the 9/11 terror attacks, I hit the road in a strategic development position with a Fortune 500 company after turning thirty, which is about ninety in record deal years. I could no longer pass as the "Lizard King of Bucks County." As an "emerging" rock star since the '90s I had three major music deals. They all tanked. Right place, wrong time. Right A&R guy, wrong label. Right son-of-a-Beatle, wrong year. Yes, I hung out with Julian Lennon while an absentee college freshman, and we actually discussed starting a band together at the now defunct BeBop Café on 8th Street in Greenwich Village, but alas, it was not to be. Mothers, do not let your sons to grow up to be . . . musicians, that is my advice, but then again, I never listened to my own mother's advice. The truth is if you are truly an artist, you have little choice in the matter but to create art, whether you aspire to win a Grammy or remain in your garage. In my case, music has been a great blessing as well as a curse, as it was decades before I saw success in the music business.

The culture of the company I worked for was hyper-conservative, so my prior ten years serving as an acolyte of Churchianity helped me to settle in organically. In retrospect, I recall the entire team were road warriors and tuned into AM right wing media all day, every day, in between long-haul calls to clients. We were all indoctrinated by Glenn Beck, Rush Limbaugh, Sean Hannity, Mark Levin, and even the darker fringe voices like Alex Jones and Michael Savage. And, in post 9/11 America, to be a patriot meant conservative and believe me, I ordered my fair share of "American Fries." Insert cringe emoji here.

A few years in I was injured on the job and subsequently terminated, because the company's perception, driven by (in)human resources was that my back was high risk for reinjury. I never returned to the road, rails, or air, AM radio, or any other job to personally line the pockets of an employer. Born and raised as an entrepreneur, it was time to live as one again. Passing on church attendance for months due to an observance of wild hypocrisy and spinelessness, which attributed to a cover-up of blatant biblical sin by local church leadership, was a decision that provided clarity and opportunity. Both decisions allowed time to convalesce and de-program (and launch my start-up company).

Part of my physical therapy included hours and hours of rac-quetball at the local gym. I always played by myself, competing with my own daily records. But something spiritual was happening during that hyper-focused activity so that the brain switched to autopi-lot as my mind began to wander into deep philosophical thoughts.

I started to ask myself: Why? Why do I believe what I believe? If I don't believe, why not? And, if I don't believe, with what do I replace that belief? Quickly falling down the rabbit hole of phi-losophizing on the meaning of life, which was nothing new, in the absence of being "informed" what to believe by right wing media or churchianitized pastors and authors for twenty plus years, I felt "born-again" again.

I clearly recall roaming Lehigh Street in a little burb north of Philly at ten, smacking down on Rain-Blo Bubble Gum trying to walk and chew gum and philosophize at the same time. Imagin-ing what the universe looked like behind the blackness of space and what that space felt like before the Big Bang and who or what caused it in the first place was perhaps a bit odd for the average ten-year-old, but to think those thoughts for the first time was pure freedom wrapped up in optimism for a future of endless possibility. Maybe I missed a calling as a theoretical physicist. Maybe not, because by twelve, all my neurons were firing on girls and dreams of rock stardom . . . and girls. Did I mention girls? "God grant me chastity and continence, but not yet," was not only St. Augustine's motto. It was clearly mine as well. Insert cringe emoji here, too.

Deprogramming myself from Churchianity offered that same child-like wonder, daring to open books by authors considered anathema to the former influencers of my life. In the process, answers to questions were uncovered that had heretofore flummoxed me (and those former influencers in my life), which was liberating.

This book was created to glue my evolved beliefs together as a form of my own therapy and understanding. I have curated a construct based on my own biblical research and drawn from countless sermons, videos, and writings of my heroes of the faith, past and present, including Irenaeus, Polycarp, St. Francis of Assisi, Father Richard Rohr, Cynthia Bourgeault, Rob Bell, Brennan Manning, Dr. Robin Parry, and Rich Mullins. But as the manuscript took shape, I realized that it could organically become helpful to those who now identify (or may soon identify) as "spiritual, but not religious"—who have left Churchianity in droves in recent years. I live in solidarity as an ally, yet still *en Christo*, as St. Paul often wrote. As noted, my intention was never to throw the baby Jesus out with the bath water and go neck deep into atheism or other religions, nor do I believe that is the intention of most who leave the corrupted and fragmented American brand of Christianity.

My prayer is that my life experience will be a blessing to everyone who comes across this little book to find some meaning in a seemingly meaningless world and a reason to carry on when life feels graceless and merciless.

It is time to transform faith. So, let's explore what an evolved faith might look like practically, logistically, corporately, and structurally. Over the course of study, we deconstructed Churchianity to reimagine a new way forward, which in full disclosure, is not new at all. In returning to our remarkable and astounding roots, forgotten to time, intentionally ignored, or practiced remotely, we can reboot the ancient "grace forward" faith for the twenty-first century.

First, let me ask you a few questions. Are you certain of your faith? Is it unwavering and steadfast? Do not be so quick to reply "yes," because it is not necessarily the best answer, and it is quite alright. Questioning your faith, the existence of God, and the meaning of life should by all means leave you with more questions than answers. Wrestling with God is OK, too. Wrestling with anyone who claims to be a Bible authority is vital to spiritual wellbeing and should throw the switch on your own study and testing of the Spirit.

True, I had a profound metaphysical experience that rattled my soul and awakened my heart to a clearer understanding of life after life. I felt God's hand on me as a young boy, searched for the meaning of life since the age of ten and researched "truth" on an intellectual level for decades. I have also struggled with missing the mark myself a time or two or ten million and include missing an authentic connection with God for years. I am no saint, yet I am, thanks to the grace of God. At the end of the day, I am only one man with more questions than answers myself. Any theologian, evangelist, pastor, or student who states otherwise is either lying to you or to him or herself.

If you claim to have more answers than questions, to put it bluntly, I question your faith. You are living more by fear than faith. Fear-based religion is a white-knuckle ride down a dead-end road of dogma, ritual, twisted nationalism, and superstition. A faith with more questions than answers is liberating and robust. I am more at peace now in the bliss of unknowing than the time spent as a fundamentalist with all the answers churchianitized for my protection. Once again, our new goal is to know deeper, not more.

God's mercy and grace are big enough to carry you through even the darkest, most heretical times of questioning. I am here to enlighten your load and will be here to continue the conversation with you and anyone who is willing to step out of their comfort zone to ask the tough questions about God and of God.

At the very least, in many ways the ingenuity of humanity has progressed since the first century and remarkably in the last one in case you had not noticed. Behold the horse drawn cart, mankind's means of transportation for the last several thousand years. Unless you are of the Amish persuasion, it was replaced a mere hundred years ago, a minor blip on the timeline of history. Voila! We can now traverse the globe in hours by air, rocket to outer space commercially, and individual mobility was transformed through the invention of automobiles and mass transit. Also, around the turn of the twentieth century, the mimeograph machine became a very big deal in that it could replicate paper copies. Today, we can literally create matter from information using 3D printers. Read that last sentence again, please. Let it sink in. Advances in medicine, technology, transportation, broadcasting, communication, logistics, and so on and so on have propelled us centuries into the future in less than one hundred years.

Yes, knowledge has exponentially increased. Wisdom has not. The fact that a doomsday clock exists in and of itself is telling. We inch ever closer to nuclear annihilation on any given day. At the time of this writing, Russian Federation President Putin is egging the US and EU on in an attempt to kickstart WWIII by way of a threatened limited strategic nuclear strike in Ukraine. War, hatred, racism, bigotry, inequality on all levels, terrorism, and horror are commonplace. The common good and common sense, not so much.

The church failed. "Bigly." Full stop. Why? Christianity was commandeered, co-opted, and subjugated by governments and authoritarians beginning with the Roman Empire, only to expand and devolve in its own corrupt centralized papal government, finally splintering into a million bits of warring but innocuous Protestant denominations and landed here: irrelevancy. Worse, it could be construed that the church is culpable in an anti-democratic US insurrection based on a perverted gospel baked into religious nationalism. Yikes.

Yet, there is hope in a rising global spiritual awakening. There is hope in the disillusionment of "faith people" who see the cracks in organized religion, but still know that they know that God is real. There is hope in a decentralized "crypto-church" focused on doing what is good and right for humanity, all humanity.

Let's focus a bit on the two major faith traditions of Christmas and Easter and the scapegoat salvation theory. I do not believe that we are required to believe in the mystical "virgin birth," the physical bodily resurrection (as we have been led to believe, that is), or the hyper Calvinist view of the atonement of Christ to fully believe in the Christ and celebrate those holidays.

The Gospel of Matthew refers to Isa 7:14 to corroborate the virgin birth of Jesus, but many scholars believe the word used, *almah* refers to simply "a girl of childbearing years, or virgin in the human sense. That is the extent of the OT prophecy, at best. The birth narrative is limited to Matthew and Luke. Mark, the oldest Gospel, does not include the miraculous story, but you would think the astonishing tale might be worth including if true. John writes that Jesus had both a mother and father but provides no birth story at all. Not believing in the miraculous conception would take nothing away from our Christmas traditions, which, to be clear, are exactly that and only that. Regardless, the birth of the savior of all mankind is still the birth of the savior of all mankind. Merry Christmas!

Next, the physical v. spiritual resurrection has been debated for two thousand years. A spiritual resurrection of Christ that appeared to humanity post crucifixion and death is equally miraculous. Resurrection from the dead, whether a physical human body or a glorified spiritual body, is still Christ conquering death, the wage of sin. Happy Easter!

Let's dig deeper. I believe there was an empty tomb. Period. I believe that Jesus died and rose as Christ. Period. But it was not a resuscitation. Jesus did not go back to live, teach, or earn a living as a carpenter in Nazareth, only to die again of old age. I believe that at the moment of resurrection, Jesus' dead physical body was transformed as incorruptible and glorified. The physical body was instantly immaterial and irrelevant. He appeared to the apostles, his extended earthly family, and finally to Paul, who describes all as "visions." In those cases, Christ needed to be recognized as Jesus.

Deeper still. The risen Jesus appears in a locked room (John 20). He travels with two followers for hours and is not recognized.

But when finally recognized, he vanishes (Luke 24). He appears in both Jerusalem (Luke and John) and Galilee (Matthew and John). He appears to Stephen in his final moments of life (Acts 7). He appears to Paul near Damascus as a brilliant light (Acts 9). He appears to John on an island off the coast of Turkey in the late 90s of the first century (Rev 1). None of these descriptions match a mortal body, nor does flesh ascend to heaven.

Regarding the atonement theory, the authoritative teachings of Jesus have a diminished value proposition when the atonement narrative is the single hyper focused driver of incarnation. For decades, the writings of Paul were used to explain Jesus. Today, the words of Jesus are required to explain Paul. It is not my intention to diminish the suffering servant as described in Isaiah, who willingly emptied his life in solidarity with mankind and rose again as the risen Christ, savior of the world, in conquering death, the wage of "sin." Just the opposite is true! Jesus clearly stated that his incarnation fulfilled the law and the prophets, but there is plenty of room for interpretation in that his death was not a scapegoat murder to appease a homicidal vengeful dad.

"Theosis," a central doctrine in Eastern Orthodox traditions, says that the fate of humanity is to become One with God. Western theology, which we discussed throughout the last chapters, was wrought and influenced by Roman civil law wherein God is judge, jury, and jailor with a bloodlust for justice. Theosis was birthed from another church father, Ireneaus, who developed the Recapitulation Theory. Irenaeus states that Christ "became what we are, that he might bring us to be even what he is himself."[1] He echoed Jesus' words in the Gospel of John 12:32: "And I, when I am lifted up from the earth, will draw all people to myself."[2] A reassuring annotation: Irenaeus was a student of Polycarp, who was a student of John, who was one of the twelve apostles of Christ and known as the "disciple whom Jesus loved."

In Recapitulation Theory, Jesus is seen as a second Adam who achieved where the first Adam failed. Healing and restoration are

1. Ireneaus, *Writings*, 55.
2. John 12:32, NIV.

the core tenets, as opposed to a penal code of substitutional atonement of original sin for the faithful and eternal retribution in hell for the lost. Thus, the incarnation of Jesus provided restoration by salvation as to what humanity lost in Adam—to be the image and likeness of God that we might recover in Christ.

We are all, theologians included, guilty of attempting to create Jesus into our own image based on personal and denominational agendas or misinterpretation. These include first-century writers, third-century Christian fathers, seventeenth-century reformers, twentieth-century Evangelicals, and postmodern New Age teachers. Today, let us make a commitment to follow Christ in his image, not ours. Jesus said, take up your cross and follow me. He is the cornerstone example of how to live: die daily to the self and give yourself to those in need of love and compassion.

Jesus did not come to start a new religion, particularly one that packs legalistic and politically conservative Jesus fans into mega churches that line the pockets of celebrity pastors, at the cost of a world in desperate need. He came to transform individuals and save the world, conquering death and sin and the law. In Christ, there is a new world, a new spiritual Adam, and a new beginning for all. As Christ transcends all religions and philosophies, true freedom, joy, grace, mercy, hope, and love have been abundantly given to all the world.

It is time to put away all the symbolic, nationalistic, and commercial trappings of religious practice and worship spectacle to engage in authentic communion with God and ourselves as oneness, which in effect costs nothing but a personal investment in time and faith. In parallel, social activism and charity in the name of Christ should be integral, performing good deeds in and on behalf of neighbors, the community, and the world.

Case in point: the overturning of Roe v. Wade and the church's culpability in that resolution, and more so its responsibility to foster the millions of additional children to be born in America in 2022 and beyond. As you recall from chapter 1, the common belief holds that the government bears no responsibility to provide such services. The responsibility lies ultimately with Churchianity when all other personal resolutions are exhausted.

Let's look at some literal numbers in a metaphorical scenario. The CDC disclosed approximately 600,000 abortions in 2021, which more than likely is vastly underreported.[3] According to shebudgets.com, it costs $225,000 to raise a child in America. The result: it will take $135,000,000,000 annually to care for these unwanted children from the ages of 0–18 born into a post-Roe world. If Churchianity shifted revenues and investments to childcare from the likes of mega churches, private jets for celebrity pastors, and 100 percent of Christian entertainment including music, film, and Christian Copyright Licensing International's "worship industrial complex," we could cough up about $40,000,000,000 leaving a $100,000,000,000 shortfall. Of course, it is unlikely that the prosperity gospel empire and its sub-culture ghetto will ever relinquish power, so yes, the scenario is preposterous and insurmountable.

Even if we could raise that kind of money or the responsibility of parenthood is opted for in vast numbers, it all ends catastrophically, and will still place 400,000 additional children in the foster care system every year. There are approximately 400,000 children in US foster care right now.[4] The overturning of Roe will exponentially burden NPOs and the US government because I'm sorry to report that the church is woefully ill-prepared for what was hoped and prayed for since the late '70s. And this scenario doesn't even touch on the abject horror to face aged-out foster care teens by the millions or the exponential increase in childhood poverty and homelessness of single parent families.

Not to be swayed by truth, math, or a concern for children once they emerge from the womb, Lynda Bell, Chair of National Right to Life, was asked to respond to a question regarding what her organization plans to do to help these mothers and children going forward in an NPR interview. She completely dodged the

3. Diamant and Mohamed, "What the Data Says," para. 6.
4. iFoster, "6 Quick Statistics," para. 1.

question, but remarked that there is already help, saying: "We are already there."[5]

I respectfully disagree. A quick poke around the National Right to Life website offers no services other than more anti-abortion propaganda, yet goes further down the rabbit hole of healthcare rationing and assisted suicide fear mongering. It notably links the distraught mother-to-be to her state website. I clicked on Pennsylvania services and noted the following solutions offered: leave your child behind at the hospital after you've given birth (so the state takes over, which goes against Churchianity's "little g" gospel as noted in chapter one), adoption (nothing new there), or parenthood. If you choose parenthood, there may or may not be an organization to help you with some diapers, formula, and temporary emergency shelter. And if you are poor enough, WIC, Medicaid, and welfare are available. Churchianity is failing in its mission out of the gate, yet again.

Simply put, there is no resolution beyond overturning Roe, albeit there were fifty years to plan. Two decades from now, I cheekily predict whatever is left of the Churchianity cult will scapegoat the millions of homeless teens roaming the streets of America and blame it all on a vast left-wing conspiracy. And lastly, if the goal is to persuade the GOP to fund $135 billion a year in government handouts, well good luck. So, in this spirit, let those of us so inclined to live out the evolved faith described in this little book step-up to the plate and come up with solutions.

We live in remarkable times, which call for intentional innovation and revolution. I cannot emphasize enough that our mission, as we career into the middle of the twenty-first century, is to know deeper, not more, which on its own merit is disruptive to the status quo. Beyond that mandate, we are to create, co-opt, and adapt technologies, enterprises, and practices to impact the world to bring hope and peace to an ever-increasingly violent and hopeless world. And to come to terms with our culpability in that hopelessness and violence.

5. NPR, "Right to Life Chair," para. 26.

Our forthright admission of guilt, our individual and collective ask of forgiveness to the entire world, and the unitive presentation of our experiential faith can and will transform the globe. This requires hand-to-hand service in trust building through love in action until the whole world can experience Christ through our lives. It will not happen until we can be trusted as the face and more importantly the hands of Jesus. We must lead by example with a servant's heart as One.

Epilogue

God's Greater Fool

"You should not fool yourself. If any of you think that you are wise by this world's standards, you should become a fool, in order to be really wise."[1] Father Richard Rohr wrote, "Wise fools are always formed in the testing ground of exile when the customary and familiar are taken away and they must go deeper and much higher for wisdom. As a result, they no longer fit or belong among their own. Yet paradoxically, they alone can point the way to the 'promised land' or the 'New Jerusalem.' Conventional wisdom is inadequate, even if widely held by good people."[2]

Father Rohr again said, "The holy fool is the last stage of the wisdom journey. It is the individual who knows their dignity and therefore does not have to polish or protect it. It is the man or woman who has true authority and does not have to defend it or anyone else's authority. It is the child of God who has met the One who watches over sparrows and fashions galaxies, and therefore can comfortably be a child of God. They and they alone can be trusted to proclaim the Reign of God."[3]

1. 1 Cor 3:18, GNT.
2. Center for Action and Contemplation, "Becoming Wise Fools," para. 2.
3. Center for Action and Contemplation, "Becoming Wise Fools," para. 4.

Followers of Churchianity will conclude that I have either been misled by the "devil disguised as light," that I am a heretic or a fool. I'm quite alright with the name calling that will castigate me behind hyper-Calvinist doctrine. I'm over it.

A "greater fool" is actually an economic term. Here's another quote from Aaron Sorkin, speaking in the voice of Sloan Sabbith from HBO's *Newsroom*, a much-underrated classic: "It's a patsy. For the rest of us to profit, we need a greater fool—someone who will buy long and sell short. Most people spend their life trying not to be the greater fool; we toss him the hot potato; we dive for his seat when the music stops. The greater fool is someone with the perfect blend of self-delusion and ego to think that he can succeed where others have failed. This whole country was made by greater fools."[4]

St. Francis of Assisi was called "God's fool" for multiple reasons including his exuberant, back-flipping joy in Christ. So then, who is "God's greater fool?"

A disciple with eyes to see and ears to hear the eternal beyond space/time. One who can sit in the peace of the Presence to "be still and know I AM God," as it is written in the Ps 46:10. A follower who attempts to believe and trust beyond normal human capacity. One who can look behind their own eyes to see Christ in everything and every person and acts accordingly with compassion, empathy, and love in action.

Am I one of God's greater fools? Hardly. On a good day I play the curmudgeon with misplaced anger. On a bad day, just stay out of my way. On a better day, I see behind my own eyes and possess a minute capacity to see Christ in all. Quick to anger at times of injustice, but quick to fall apart in tears at the slightest glint of the authentic tragic beauty of humanity. In a word, I am a hot mess like everyone else, and in no position to judge. Neither is any other human alive or dead on this planet, save for Christ.

I, like most, have little patience for patience and have been known to joke about patience in my impatience saying, "How can we call Patience virtuous? She is such a tease." Love may be patient

4. Mottola, "Greater Fool."

and patience may be a virtue, but I struggle daily with both. I am a work in progress, and so are you.

We are all in the same boat, baptized into the civilization, culture, family, environment, and the DNA of our ancestry, which leads to our tribe, whether adopted or preordained by individual predisposition. And I am using our biblical definition of baptism, not sprinkled, not dunked, but completely soaked through to the bone, and water-logged. These are not surface stains to be washed away with bleach or holy water. All this baggage we tow like pack mules, carrying the weight of the world on our shoulders. All of us. Everyone. Every single day.

How then can we break free? How can we acquire eyes that see behind and beyond our own eyes? Minute by minute, hour by hour, day by day, week by week, year by year, decade by decade each one of us exists in the shallows of ego, culture, and civilization's accoutrements. Why? Because we either don't believe we can swim in the deep end or even know it exists or maybe we falsely believe we've been in the deep end all along.

The truth: our collective existence is merely a human construct. Thus, when we begin to know that we know that oneness with God, or that the kingdom of God is within, even superficially, it will cause a paradigm shift, and on that day, we will change. Each of us will break free to dive in the fathoms of the unfathomable to see a whole new world of possibilities, floating unencumbered in the murky mystery of the never-ending love of God.

In postmodern vernacular, to follow Christ as a disciple, being disciplined to follow the teachings of Christ, leading by his example, teaching the world about Jesus, and acting in love to positively impact the globe might be coined "love leader." Let's say I just did.

Maybe it's time to remove labels altogether. Ripe for disruption, perhaps eradicating labels like "church" and "Christian" would benefit everybody. Early followers of Christ followed The Way. The term "Christian," which meant "little Christs," was derogatorily pushed on followers of The Way by mockers of the time.

So, let's not get caught up in names anymore. Thus, if one wanted to rid oneself of all religious trappings, while remaining *en Christo*, as spiritual but not religious, living free indeed, one would become a "love leader," regardless of monikers. Let's go big to transform the world with a radically diverse, equitable, inclusive, engaged, authentic, IRL (in real life), and digital global community of love leaders, committed to creating a better world in the image of Christ's love. A "saved" world where man's inhumanity to man can evolve to man's divinity to man. No, not that man is God, let's not get trapped in semantics. We are way beyond that now, aren't we? I am simply making a construct out of a hopeful future, which we could all use right about now.

Love leaders will create a global community for all humanity seeking spiritual meaning to their lives, while engaging in activities to change the world for good with compassion and love. I am compelled and driven to create such a community of truth seekers. To that end, a massive collaborative effort is in play in the building of "charismata," which loosely translated from Greek means "grace in action."

Imagine a digital global intentional community of post-evangelicals and seekers of truth from all walks of life asking tough questions, exploring teachings and science, living as One, where politics are checked at the door along with egos, with justice and peace sought for all, and radically DEI (diverse, equitable, and inclusive). Civil discourse practiced in a safe space unencumbered by tribalism and warring factions, while collaborative projects positively impact individuals, local communities, and the world. That is what we are building right now. And that is just one example of how together, we can exorcise "Mere Churchianity" to awaken to the fullness of love, which is very good news indeed.

Join us at www.TheFullnessOfLove.com.

Peace of Christ to you.

Bibliography

Balmer, Randel. "The Real Origins of the Religious Right. They'll Tell You It Was Abortion. Sorry, the Message Is Clear: It Was Segregation." *Politico Magazine*, May 27, 2014. www.politico.com/magazine/story/2014/05/religious-right-real-origins-107133/.

Barna. "How We Got Here: Spiritual and Political Profiles of America." *Barna Group* (Blog), May 23, 2017. www.barna.com/research/got-spiritual-political-profiles-america/.

Bell, Rob. *Jesus Wants to Save Christians*. Grand Rapids, MI: Zondervan, 2008.

———. *Love Wins*. New York: Harper Collins, 2011.

Bourgeault, Cynthia. "Go Beyond the Mind, Lesson 13." Cynthia Bourgeault (Blog), May 18, 2021. cynthiabourgeault.org/2021/05/18/go-beyond-mind/.

Brockman, David R. "The Radical Theology that Can Make Religious Freedom a Thing of the Past." *Texas Observer*, June 2, 2016. www.texasobserver.org/dominion-theology/.

Center for Action and Contemplation. "Becoming Wise Fools." February 26, 2021. cac.org/daily-meditations/becoming-wise-fools-2021-02-26/.

———. "Changing Our Minds." March 29, 2016. cac.org/daily-meditations/changing-our-minds-2016-03-29/.

Corrigan, Kevin, and L. Michael Harrington. "Pseudo-Dionysius the Areopagite." *Stanford Encyclopedia of Philosophy* (Winter 2019). plato.stanford.edu/archives/win2019/entries/pseudo-dionysius-areopagite/.

Diamant, Jeff, and Besheer Mohamed. "What the Data Says About Abortion in the U.S." Pew Research Center, June 24, 2022. pewresearch.org/fact-tank/2022/06/24/what-the-data-says-about-abortion-in-the-u-s-2/.

Bibliography

Elwell, Walter A. *Evangelical Dictionary of Theology*. Grand Rapids, MI: Baker, 2001.

Faulk Frank. "Biocentrism: Rethinking Time, Space, Consciousness, and the Illusion of Death." CBC Radio, September 20, 2018. https://www.cbc.ca/radio/ideas/biocentrism-rethinking-time-space-consciousness-and-the-illusion-of-death-1.3789414.

Floyd, Alex. "The Radical Right: The Racist Origins of the Christian Right Wing." *Brown Political Review*, October 24, 2015. https://www.brownpoliticalreview.org/2015/10/the-racial-right-the-racist-origins-of-the-christian-right-wing/.

Frieden, Ken. "The Language of Demonic Possession: A Key-Word Analysis." *Religion* 58 (1990). https://surface.syr.edu/rel/58

Galli, Mark. "Trump Should Be Removed from Office." *Christianity Today*, December 19, 2019. https://www.christianitytoday.com/ct/2019/december-web-only/trump-should-be-removed-from-office.html.

GMA Dove Awards. "1998 Rich Mullins Tribute." *YouTube*, January 29, 2014. www.youtube.com/watch?v=NNra3f8Hslo.

iFoster. "6 Quick Statistics on the Current State of Foster Care." iFoster, November 9, 2020. https://www.ifoster.org/blogs/6-quick-statistics-on-the-current-state-of-foster-care/.

Ireneus. *The Writings of Ireneus*. Translated by Rev. Alexander Roberts and Rev. W. H. Rambert. London: T & T Clark, 1869.

Harding, James E. "Enochic Judaism: Three Defining Paradigm Exemplars/The Enoch-Metatron Tradition." *Journal of Biblical Literature* 125 (Fall 2006) 587–92.

Justia US Law. *Green v. Connally*. 330 F. Supp.1150 (DDC 1971) June 30, 1971. law.justia.com/cases/federal/district-courts/FSupp/330/1150/2126265/.

Kelly, Henry Ansgar. *Satan: A Biography*. Cambridge: Cambridge University Press, 2006. https://books.google.com/books?id=gPIpQgolRbMC&q=intitle:satan+inauthor:kelly&pg=PA12#v=onepage&q&f=false.

Kraley, Shon H. "Neoplatonic Influences in Augustine's Confessions." *Anthós* 1.1 (1990) 47–50. pdxscholar.library.pdx.edu/cgi/viewcontent.cgi?article=1010&context=anthos_archives.

Merton, Thomas. *New Seeds of Contemplation*. New York: New Directions, 2007. maryourhelp.org/e-books/catholic-ebooks/catholic-ebooks2.html.

Mottola, Greg, dir. "The Greater Fool." *The Newsroom*, season 1, episode 10, HBO, August 26, 2012.

Mullins, Rich. "Rich Mullins Quote." In Concert, Lufkin, Texas, July 19, 1997. Libquotes, n.d. https://libquotes.com/rich-mullins/quote/lbi9k2h.

New World Encyclopedia contributors. "Manichaeism." New World Encyclopedia, August 9, 2018. newworldencyclopedia.org/p/index.php?title=Manichaeism&oldid=1013647.

NPR. "The Right to Life Chair Responds to Overturning Federal Abortion Rights." *All Things Considered*, June 24, 2022. https://www.npr.org/2022/06/24/1107531700/right-to-life-chair-responds-to-overturning-of-federal-abortion-rights.

Bibliography

Patterson, John JP. "Rob Bell: Jesus, Domitian and The Book of Revelation." *YouTube*, May 16, 2018. www.youtube.com/watch?v=uThyuSy8CsM.

Basu-Ray, Indranill. "Consciousness: The Scientific and Yogic View-Complementary Not Adversarial." *Times of India* (Blog), September 12, 2021. timesofindia.indiatimes.com/blogs/basu-rays-rabid-talks/consciousness-the-scientific-and-yogic-view-complementary-not-adversarial/.

Rohr, Richard. *The Naked Now: Learning to See as the Mystics See.* New York: Crossroad, 2009.

Shapero, Hannah M. G. "Zoroastrianism, Judaism, and Christianity." Osher Lifelong Learning Institute, George Mason Univerity, September 6, 1997. https://olli.gmu.edu/docstore/600docs/1403-651-3-Zoroastrianism,%20Judaism,%20and%20Christianity.pdf.

Sopelsa, Brooke. "Trump Cabinet's Bible Teacher Says Gays Cause God's Wrath in Covid-19 Blog Post." *NBC News*, March 25, 2020. https://www.nbcnews.com/feature/nbc-out/trump-s-bible-teacher-says-gays-among-those-blame-covid-n1168981.

Stewart, Katherine. *The Power Worshipers: Inside the Dangerous Rise of Religious Nationalism.* New York: Bloomsbury, 2019.

Taliesin, Julia. "Profile on the Right: The Heritage Foundation." Political Research Associates, June 22, 2018. politicalresearch.org/2018/06/22/profile-right-heritage-foundation.

Tranquillus, Gaius Suetonius. *The Lives of the Twelve Caesars.* Vol. 12, *Titus Flavius Domitianus (Domitian).* Translated by Alexander Thompson. New Haven, CT: Aeterna, 2022.

Uebersax, John. "St. Macrina's Exegesis of the Parable of the Sower." Christian Platonism (Blog), July 12, 2017. https://catholicgnosis.wordpress.com/2017/07/12/st-macrina-sower/.

9 781666 740967